W9-CNZ-058

CONTINENTAL CRUCIBLE

CONTINENTAL CRUCIBLE

Big Business, Workers and Unions in the Transformation of North America

Richard Roman & Edur Velasco Arregui

Fernwood Publishing • Halifax & Winnipeg

To our parents, immigrants to the Americas,
who believed that another world was possible.

Copyright © 2013 Richard Roman and Edur Velasco Arregui

All rights reserved. No part of this book may be reproduced or transmitted in
any form by any means without permission in writing from the publisher,
except by a reviewer, who may quote brief passages in a review.

Editing: Curran Faris
Text design: Brenda Conroy
Cover design: John van der Woude
Printed and bound in Canada by Hignell Book Printing

Published in Canada by Fernwood Publishing
32 Oceanvista Lane, Black Point, Nova Scotia, B0J 1B0
and 748 Broadway Avenue, Winnipeg, Manitoba, R3G 0X3
www.fernwoodpublishing.ca

Fernwood Publishing Company Limited gratefully acknowledges the financial support
of the Government of Canada through the Canada Book Fund and the Canada Council
for the Arts, the Nova Scotia Department of Communities, Culture and Heritage,
the Manitoba Department of Culture, Heritage and Tourism under the
Manitoba Publishers Marketing Assistance Program and the Province of Manitoba,
through the Book Publishing Tax Credit, for our publishing program.

Library and Archives Canada Cataloguing in Publication

Roman, Richard
Continental crucible: big business, workers and unions in the transformation of North America /
Richard Roman and Edur Velasco Arregui.

Includes bibliographical references and index.
ISBN 978-1-55266-547-3

1. Labor unions—North America. 2. Corporate power--North America. 3. Labor movement—
North America.4. Workingclass—North America—Social conditions. 5. Free trade—Economic
aspects—North America. 6. North America—Commerce. I. Velasco Arregui, Edur II. Title.

HF1746.R64 2013   331.88097   C2012-908258-9

Contents

Acronyms and Abbreviations

ACCM	American Chamber of Commerce of Mexico
ACTPN	Advisory Committee on Trade Policy and Negotiations
AFL	American Federation of Labor
AFL-CIO	American Federation of Labor-Congress of Industrial Organizations
ASARCO	American Smelting and Refining Company
BCNI	Business Council on National Issues
BCTD	Building and Construction Trades Department
BCTF	British Columbia Teachers Federation
BFA	Bilateral Framework Agreement on Trade and Investment
BIP	Border Industrialization Program
BLS	Bureau of Labour Statistics
BRT	Business Roundtable
CATJO	Canadian Alliance for Trade and Job Opportunities
CAUT	Canadian Association of University Teachers
CAW	Canadian Auto Workers
CCC	Canadian Chamber of Commerce
CCCE	Canadian Council of Chief Executives
CCE	Consejo Coordinador Empresarial (Business Co-ordinating Council)
CDC	Canada Development Corporation
CEMAI	Consejo Empresarial Mexicano para Asuntos Internacionales (Mexican Business Council for International Affairs)
CIO	Congress of Industrial Organizations
CLC	Canadian Labour Congress
CMA	Canadian Manufacturers' Association
CMHN	Cámara Mexicana de Hombres de Negocios (Mexican Businessmen's Council)
COECE	Coordinadora de Organismos Empresarios de Comercio Exterior (Coordinator for Foreign Trade Business Organizations)
CPP	Canada Pension Plan
CPQ	Le Conseil du patronat du Québec (Quebec Council of Employers)
COM	Casa del Obrero Mundial (House of the World Workers)
CONEVAL	Consejo Nacional de Evaluación de la Política de Desarrollo Social (National Council for the Evaluation of Social Development Policy)
CSQ	Confédération des syndicats du Québec (Confederation of Trade Unions of Quebec)
CT	Congreso del Trabajo (Labour Congress)
CTF	Canadian Teachers' Federation
CTM	Confederación de Trabajadores de México (Confederation of Mexican Workers)
CUAIR	Construction Users Anti-Inflation Roundtable
CUFTA	Canada–U.S. Free Trade Agreement
ERISA	Employee Retirement Income Security Act
FAT	Frente Auténtico del Trabajo (Authentic Workers' Front)

FDN	Frente Democrático Nacional (National Democratic Front)
FIRA	Foreign Investment Review Agency
FLQ	Front de libération du Québec (Quebec Liberation Front)
FNEEQ-CSN	Fédération nationale des enseignantes et des enseignants du Québec
GDP	gross domestic product
ICA	Ingenieros Civiles Asociados (Civil Engineers Associates)
IMF	International Monetary Fund
IMSS	Instituto Mexicano del Seguro Social (Mexican Social Security Institute)
INEGI	Instituto Nacional de Estadística Geografica e Informática (National Institute of Statistic, Geography and Computing)
ISI	import substitution industrialization
ISSSTE	Instituto de Seguridad y Servicios Sociales de los Trabajadores del Estado (Institute for Social Security and Services for State Workers)
IWW	Industrial Workers of the World (Wobblies)
LIUNA	Laborers International Union of North America
LLSG	Labor Law Study Group
MEXUS	Mexico–U.S. Business Committee
MTS	Manitoba Teachers' Society
NAALC	North American Agreement on Labor Cooperation
NAFTA	North American Free Trade Agreement
NAM	National Association of Manufacturers
NDP	New Democratic Party
NEP	National Energy Program
NFIB	National Federation of Independent Businesses
NGA	National Governors Association
NSBA	National Small Businesses Association
OBU	One Big Union
OSHA	Occupation Health and Safety Act
OSSTF	Ontario Secondary School Teachers Federation
OSW	Occupy Wall Street
PACs	Political Action Committees
PAN	Partido Acción Nacional (National Action Party)
PRD	Partido de la Revolución Democrática (Party of the Democratic Revolution)
PRI	Partido Revolucionario Institucional (Institutional Revolutionary Party)
SBLC	Small Business Legislative Council
SNTMMSRM	Sindicato Nacional de Trabajadores Mineros, Metalúrgicos, Siderúrgicos y Similares de la República Mexicana (National Union of Mine and Metal Workers of the Mexican Republic, Los Mineros, Mexican Miners Union)
TAGs	trade advisory groups
TNSA	Trinational Solidarity Alliance
UAW	United Auto Workers
UE	United Electrical, Radio & Machine Workers of America
USW	United Steel Workers
WEF	World Economic Forum

Acknowledgements

This book grew out of a project conceived almost twenty years ago when we met at a conference on NAFTA in Toronto. Our plan was to write a quick, little book on the peculiarities of Mexican unions that would serve as a guide to Canadian and U.S. labour activists in their relations with Mexican workers in the new world of NAFTA. The project grew and grew in scope. This book, which focuses on continental aspects of class struggle in North America, is one of the outcomes of the project. The other aspect of the project, the historical analysis of the formation of the Mexican working class and Mexican unions, is soon to be completed, though aspects of it have been published as articles. The original project not only grew in scope but was interrupted many times by political, union and personal events.

We are deeply indebted to our parents who brought the revolutionary democratic traditions of the sailors' councils of the Spanish Civil War and those of the Jewish Labour Bund of Lithuania, Poland and Russia with them to the Americas. We thank them for passing on their belief in the immense potential of ordinary working people to create a new world of justice, equality and genuine democracy. We have dedicated this book to them — Federico Velasco Koba (1914–74), Begoña Arregui Azkarate (1923–), Julius Roman (née Romatsky, 1884–1957), and Sarah Roman (née Borkofsky, 1904–76).

Dick would like to thank his wife, Jo Anne Maikawa, and his sons, Zev and Nathaniel, for their support and faith in the project, not only of the book, but of the struggle of working people to make another world possible. There are so many people to thank for encouragement and enlightenment along all these years but only room to mention a handful. Harvey Freedman and Ed Silva for being great coaches, Art Lipow for his enthusiastic support since the beginning of the project, Stephan Dobson for intellectual assistance and Paul Fraschetti for numerous computer rescue missions.

Edur would like to thank his family as well as his friends, colleagues and *compañeros*, too numerous to mention, for their support and encouragement.

We have learned much from discussions with Rafael Mayoral and Gabriel Mendoza. We owe a special thanks to Alejandro Alvárez and Mel Watkins, two of the most insightful analysts of North American integration, for their generous intellectual support over many years.

We also thank Wayne Antony of Fernwood Publishing and the two anonymous reviewers for their incisive critiques of the original manuscript. We thank Wayne as well for his enthusiastic support and the staff at Fernwood for their help in guiding the book through its various stages of production — Curran Faris, Beverley Rach, Brenda Conroy, Nancy Malek and John van der Woude

This book has been published with the help of a grant from the Canadian Federation for the Humanities and Social Sciences, through the Awards to Scholarly Publications Program, using funds provided by the Social Sciences and Humanities Research Council of Canada.

Preface

On January 1, 1994, the North American Free Trade Agreement (NAFTA), between United States, Canada and Mexico came into effect. A novel feature was that it included Mexico within the economic region of North America by, in effect, incorporating it into the Canada–United States Free Trade Agreement that had been implemented only five years earlier. This was clearly an event of some significance.

Like the inquisitive child, the first question that is likely to occur to us is: Why has this happened? It is, of course, the kind of question to which there can be no simple answer. Ask a historian such a question and he or she is likely to reply that it is the result of "a conjuncture of circumstances." Fortunately, there is a simpler way to approach this dilemma. We should ask who did it, who made it happen and who dealt the deck and held the trump cards.

In this well documented and very accessible book, Richard Roman and Edur Velasco Arregui give a straightforward and convincing answer: big business, or capital, in each country, acting and interacting separately and together. In today's lingo, we call them the "one-percenters." In close alliance with their states, they exercise power.

Power gets its way. Free trade may have that sound of the good and the innocuous about it, but trade agreements in fact are bills of rights — in the Canadian terminology, Charters of Rights and Freedoms — for corporations. Already dominating, power is further entrenched, both nationally and continentally. The most telling provision is the requirement for "national treatment," which means that each state must treat the corporations of the other two countries as if they were their own.

Power reaps its rewards; take note of the increasing maldistribution of income in the past two decades in all three countries. And, in the nature of things, power gets good press.

Still, that is only half the story. At every step of the way, there is resistance, from labour — from working people and their unions — and from civil society, from the "ninety-nine-percenters," who sense that they will pay a price for the bill of goods they are being sold. The greatest merit of this book is its thorough documentation of this for all three countries.

I speak with some feeling on this matter. In 1987 and 1988, on leave from my university, I worked as an advisor on free trade to the pan-Canadian trade union federation, the Canadian Labour Congress. The Congress opposed the proposed Canada–United States Free Trade Agreement, which then morphed into NAFTA, on behalf of its members while working closely within a coalition that included social activists, environmentalists, feminists, Canadian nationalists and Indigenous people. The national election of late 1988 turned into a debate about free trade. It was a close election, but capital won.

The struggle, however, goes on, as we have seen most recently in the Occupy movement. Our authors, being themselves activists as well as scholars, know that. Their special insight is to see that once power has explicitly defined the terrain as continental or trinational, labour in its numerous manifestations can do the same. They tell us about where this is happening and how it might be made to happen more.

This book is their plea, the plea of engaged and hopeful intellectuals. Read and heed.

— *Mel Watkins, Professor Emeritus of Economics and Political Science, University of Toronto and Adjunct Research Professor, Institute of Political Economy, Carleton University*

Introduction

The Crucible of North American Transformation

The crucible of North American transformation is heating up, but its outcome is far from clear. There is a growing clash between those pushing to continue the corporate neo-liberal offensive and the movements of resistance. The same powerful forces that unleashed the neo-liberal transformation of North America are now using the economic crisis as their new rationale for intensifying their offensive. The deepening attack on public sector unions in Mexico, the United States and Canada, as well as the ongoing cuts to social spending, reflects the continuation of the offensive started by big business forty years ago. The labour movement in the United States, Canada and Mexico responded to the big business offensive through tactics and strategies that had been consolidated during a period of the "social contract," the period in which capital in some sectors accepted unions and rising wages and benefits in exchange for labour peace and uninterrupted production . But while capital was tearing the social pacts to shreds, the labour movement struggled to hold them together by methods that no longer worked in these new conditions.

The big business transformation of the continent has shown time and again that the old methods of competition among different sectors of the working class for jobs has led to a downward cycle of concessions from workers and rising subsidies to big business from government. This transformation has shown that solidarity needs to replace competition among the continental and global working class in order to challenge the capitalist offensive. The fight against the economic treaties, especially NAFTA (North American Free Trade Agreement), opened new channels of communication among unions and started them on a path of exploring new and deeper forms of solidarity.

Yet, the corporate offensive has also sown the seeds of resistance both by the intensification of hardship and suffering and by the unintended promotion of cross-border working-class links. The three working classes have two sets of overlapping but distinct binational working-class relationships. The Mexican working class is deeply rooted in its own labour market as well as that of the U.S.; continental economic integration has consolidated its binational (U.S.–Mexico) character even further. And many, if not most, workers in the private sector in Canada and the U.S. are members of "international" unions, unions that are actually Canadian–U.S. binational unions. These two working-class, binational relationships contain the seeds for a potential trinational or continental fightback against the trinational corporate offensive.

This ongoing transformation of each of the countries in North America has created an arena of struggle which can only be understood from a perspective that combines a broad class-struggle approach with a pan-continental approach.

Big business in all three countries sought to lock in their domestic neo-liberal reforms through so-called free trade agreements: the Canada–U.S. Free Trade Agreement (CUFTA — January 1, 1989) and the North American Free Trade Agreement (NAFTA — January 1, 1994). In the words of Ambassador Jaime Zabludovsky of Mexico, NAFTA made "economic reforms permanent and, thus, extended the planning horizons for domestic and foreign investors" (Grayson 2007: xi). All three capitalist classes sought to secure and expand the playing field for investments and continentally integrated production and markets. The geographical expansion of "safe" investment areas allowed for an intensification of the downward harmonization of wages, working conditions and benefits already taking place domestically in all three countries. As well, U.S. big business and the U.S. state sought to gain secure access to the natural resources of Canada and Mexico.

The devastation of millions of lives in Canada, Mexico and the United States did not start with the 2008 financial crisis — it started at different moments in the late 1960s and 1970s as a response to workers' militancy, governmental flirtation with economic nationalism in Canada and Mexico, declining profits and increased global competition. Key members of big business in each country decided to try to organize their class to turn things around. They have spent vast sums of money in carrying out a multi-faceted offensive in their class interests. To date, the capitalist classes have had great success in their deliberate aim to degrade the labour markets.

The success of this offensive required the development of a common perspective, relative unity and a shared agenda within the capitalist class, to which the political and state elites were won over or compelled to impose on the whole society. The pluralism of capitalist voices and their disagreements about social issues does not belie their unity on fundamental class issues on a perspective that has come to be known as neo-liberalism. The key objectives in the neo-liberal offensive of the last several decades have been 1) the creation of a cheaper and more pliable labour force, 2) the transfer of public funds and services to private hands, involving pensions, housing, power, transportation, education and health care and 3) the appropriation of all profitable natural resources by business. Under neo-liberalism, business is to be given free reign to do as it sees fit, while the coercive role of the state over the working class and society in general is increased.

The largest corporations in each of these countries organized new associations that developed understandings and policies that have become the new "common sense" of the political elites, the media and some sectors of the population. In Canada, the new organization was the Business Council on National Issues (BCNI), which was formed in 1976 and later renamed the Canadian Council of Chief Executives (CCCE). In the United States, the new organization was called the Business Roundtable (BRT), organized in 1972. In Mexico, it was the Consejo Coordinador Empresarial (CCE, Business Co-ordinating Council), which was formed in 1975 and was largely controlled by a smaller, even more elite organization, the Consejo Mexicana de Hombres de Negocios (CMHN, Mexican Businessmen's Council), which had been formed in 1962. These organizations were the core of a much broader movement of capitalists whose goal was to take society in a neo-liberal direction. In concert with each other, these organizations were the main force behind the free trade agreements: CCCE and BRT developed the foundations of CUFTA, and CCE and BRT were the forces behind NAFTA. These organizations continue to play central roles in the attempts to promote deeper continental integration.

The two sets of binational working-class relationships provide a platform for the development of trinational or continental worker resistance to the corporate neo-liberal offensive. However, there are many obstacles to effective resistance posed by the neo-liberal offensive and the existing character of unionism in each of the countries. Unionism, developed in earlier epochs of capitalism in each country, is presently not capable of mounting effective worker mobilization and resistance to the downward harmonization of neo-liberalism. Unions need to be transformed into more democratic, participatory and politically independent organizations that promote a wider and deeper notion of solidarity, a notion more suitable to the current globalized character of capitalism.

The Mexican reality has important implications for continental development in general and for the prospects of labour solidarity more specifically. The continental integration promoted by NAFTA brought together an explosive "third world" country with two relatively stable capitalist democracies. The struggles of the Mexican working class take place in the context of a country with multiple, deep crises: the drug war, the long organic crisis of the old regime and the crisis of the Mexican economy and the lack of jobs. The dire needs of Mexican workers and the extremely difficult and volatile context of their struggles means that a radicalization of class conflict is even more likely to occur and to be more extreme in Mexico than elsewhere in North America. The transnational character of the Mexican working class has the potential to be the spark of a North American labour insurgency, both through the spill-over effects and through the example of struggle.

The corporate assault is forcing workers and unions in all three countries to look for more effective ways of fighting back. There is a growing awareness among workers that the struggle needs to be continental, if not global. The two sets of long-existing binational working-class relations could provide the core elements for building a continental labour movement, one that could create new and more effective forms of national, binational, and trinational struggle. Some of the elements of a new continental workers' movement can be glimpsed in the cross-border workers' mobilizations of 2006 and the formation of working relations between some Mexican, Canadian and U.S. unions. These elements can be the building blocks for a continental, class-wide, transformational workers' movement that could challenge the big business transformation of North America. Another North America is possible.

PART I

THE BIG BUSINESS OFFENSIVE

Continental Integration and
the Class Offensive from Above

Chapter 1

The North American Corporate Offensive
The United States

The deterioration of labor relations in our industry has progressed to the point that the very existence of the construction industry as a free enterprise is in jeopardy. In fact, its impact is so far reaching that it poses a threat to our entire economic system. — John Graney, labor relations manager of Ebasco Services, NCA (National Constructors Association), past president and future Roundtable official (speaking in 1968, cited in Linder 2000: 231)

About Us

Business Roundtable (BRT) is an association of chief executive officers of leading U.S. companies with more than $7.3 trillion in annual revenues and nearly 16 million employees. BRT member companies comprise nearly a third of the total value of the U.S. stock market and invest more than $150 billion annually in research and development — equal to 61 percent of U.S. private R&D spending. Our companies pay $182 billion in dividends to shareholders and generate nearly $500 billion in sales for small and medium-sized businesses annually. BRT companies give more than $9 billion a year in combined charitable contributions.

Business Roundtable was established in 1972, founded on the belief that in a pluralistic society, businesses should play an active and effective role in the formation of public policy.

Uniting and amplifying the diverse business perspectives and voices of America's top CEOs, Business Roundtable innovates and advocates to help expand economic opportunity for all Americans.

Business Roundtable's effectiveness is rooted in the direct, personal participation of its CEO members, who present government with reasoned alternatives and positive policy suggestions. Business Roundtable identifies issues early, employs careful research and understands the problems faced by government as well as business. (Business Roundtable n.d.)

Class war is unceasing in a capitalist society. But the economic expansion that continued for several decades after World War II allowed sections of business, however reluctantly, to share their profits with workers in exchange for labour peace. These truces in the class war took place when specific firms and industrial sectors calculated that labour peace was more profitable than open conflict. The post-World War II period in the U.S. was one in which firms in oligopolistic sectors, sectors controlled by a few producers — automobile producers being the most salient example — were willing to trade off some wage concessions and company-based social wages (health care and pension plans, for example) — the costs of which they could pass on to consumers — for shop-floor control and uninterrupted production. But for much of the rest of the economy, the more brutal war against workers and unions continued uninterrupted (Ross and Trachte 1990). There were always sectors of capital that bitterly fought against unions and a social wage out of various mixes of interest and ideology. As Phillips-Fein shows in her book, *Invisible Hands: The Businessmen's Crusade against the New Deal* (2009), there were sectors of U.S. capital that never accepted the social reforms and union rights that accompanied the New Deal. There was, as there always is, a plurality of interests and perspectives within the capitalist class, and there was no broad class consensus on strategies towards unions and the role of the state in the economy. This would begin to change with the social and political turmoil of the 1960s and most especially with the rising militancy of workers in the 1960s and early 1970s, a militancy that achieved significant wage gains for key, unionized sectors of the working class.

The concessions that labour militancy forced from sectors of capital were made possible by both the expansionary character of post-World War II capitalism and the oligopolistic character of certain industries. But this situation began to change in the late 1960s and early 1970s. The growth of competition from Europe and Asia put pressure on U.S. corporations while, at the same time, the tight labour market of the late 1960s gave workers and unions more confidence and combativeness. The rise and triumph of the corporate neoliberal agenda did not simply happen because of "market forces" or globalization." The most powerful corporations in the U.S. — many of them the most powerful in the world — organized to make it happen; they developed their own consensus and mobilized their vast resources and networks to *make* it happen. They were determined to counter the surge in labour militancy and reverse the wage gains that took place in the 1960s and peaked during the last phase of the Vietnam War in 1969–71. The corporate offensive was not only aimed at constraining workers' militancy and reducing wage gains, it was also a response to the challenge that seemed to be posed by the various protest movements of the 1960s, movements that appeared threatening to the status quo and had resonances among young and Black workers.

Several overlapping streams of capitalist thought and organization developed in the 1960s and 1970s that would begin the process of uniting capitalists in a deeper and more determined war against workers. Various conservative intellectuals and some far-sighted capitalists bemoaned the divided nature of capitalist responses to workers and unions as well as the narrow economic focus of many capitalists. They called for a united capitalist effort to reshape society and culture. One of the early currents to emerge was a group initiated by Douglas Soutar of American Smelting and Refining Company (presently known as ASARCO, LLL) and Virgil Day of General Electric that brought together what Soutar called "thought leaders" from "very big blue chip companies" to begin winning business leaders to a new perspective (Gross 1995: 201). This effort led to the formation of the Labor Law Study Group (LLSG), which was initially chaired by Fred Atkinson, senior vice-president of R.H. Macy and Co. They were joined by nine other top corporate labour relations people who came from AT&T, Ford, U.S. Steel, Union Carbide, General Dynamics, B.F. Goodrich, Humble Oil and Refining, Columbia Gas System Service and Sears Roebuck (Gross 1995: 365, note 71):

> These men were selected, according to Soutar, because they had "clout," belonged to "all the trade associations in every nook and cranny in the country," worked for corporations with "billions of dollars" and had expertise in labor-management relations. The chief executive officers of these companies gave their financial support, but the corporate heads of labor relations, positions that did not exist in most companies until the mid-1950s, did the work. Calling itself the "No-Name Committee" or "Nothing Committee" because it originally had no authority or portfolio, the twelve (known in inner management circles as "the Twelve Apostles) set about solidifying support from their own firms, bringing in many other companies and trade association, getting funding, and establishing a supervisory relationship with Chamber of Commerce staffers responsible for drafting legislative proposals. (Gross 1995: 201–2)

Soutar later co-founded what became the key U.S. capitalist organization, the Business Round Table (BRT) and chaired its Labor-Management Committee. Soutar and Day understood that the climate of public opinion had to be transformed, that the ideological hegemony of business involved both unity within their class and changing popular consciousness. The increasing international competition faced by U.S. business and the political and social turmoil of the 1960s would provide powerful pushes towards uniting business in a deeper class struggle perspective, a perspective that has come to be called "neo-liberalism."

The LLSG had formed in the mid-1960s as a way of attacking worker and union rights. As well, the LLSG was seen by its founders as a way of uniting business around a common cause of, in the words of one if its founders, "exorcizing the NLRB [National Labor Relations Board]" (Gross 1995: 201). In other words, the attack on the NLRB, whose decisions often incensed corporations, would be the way in which business would develop more unity and thus be able to water down, if not eliminate, governmental protection of workers and unions. The LLSG hired the world's largest public relations firm, Hill and Knowlton, to manipulate public opinion, all the while seeking to keep their committee and its composition secret:

> Hill and Knowlton feared that its work would be undermined if the existence and identity of the Labor Law Reform Group was discovered and made public by unfriendly forces that could portray the reform project as the instrument of a reactionary employer group. The LLRG, however, decided against revealing its identity or discussing publicly the work of those participating in the project. In part, the steering committee was heeding the wisdom of its adviser, Senator Everett Dirksen "to keep a very low profile." "Keep out of sight," Dirksen warned, "because, if anybody learns you're doing this drafting, you're going to be smeared and reviled and the labor guys will take care of you in a hurry." As Soutar recalled, "we were always behind the scenes; we didn't want to get too prominent." (Gross 1995: 207)

Hill and Knowlton proposed a multi-faceted approach for turning public opinion against unions. The strategy they proposed included providing anti-union story outlines and data to writers for prestigious magazines, supplying anti-union materials to school textbook writers, preparing anti-union editorials that could be used by newspapers, influencing TV comedy shows to present unions in an unfavorable light and even trying to get anti-union content into nationally syndicated comic strips. (Gross 1995: 208). The plan was acceptable to the LLRG but it is unclear which, if any, parts of it were implemented. (Gross 1995: 368, note 115). But the temporary alliance between President Nixon and the American Federation of Labor-Congress of Industrial Organizations (AFL-CIO) leadership over the war in Vietnam blocked their short-term efforts to transform the NLRB and labour law, forcing them to focus for a period on influencing the selection of members to the NLRB until the political situation improved for their goals of a deeper transformation (Gross 1995: 217–18; Linder 2000).

The labour militancy of the late 1960s and early 1970s had also led to the organization of another key and powerful business class organization, the Construction Users Anti-Inflation Roundtable (CUAIR). The CUAIR was organized by big industrial capitalists (including those in the oil and gas industry) with the aim of breaking unions, reducing costs and increasing labour discipline in the construction industry. The formation of the CUAIR was a response to the fear that successful militancy among construction workers would lead to an escalation of demands by other industrial workers as well as a concern about rising construction costs, which increased the capital costs of industrial firms and resource companies. In November 1968, shortly after Richard Nixon had been elected President, the U.S. Chamber of Commerce held the "National Conference on Construction Problems," at which a task force on problems in the construction industry was set up. In April 1969, the National Association of Manufacturers (NAM) published a report called "Chaos in the Construction Industry." The CUAIR itself was formed in May 1969, and its leaders soon met with top officials of the Nixon administration, even before its very existence had been announced publicly. The CUAIR was made up exclusively of presidents of companies, chairmen of boards and CEOs. By February 1970, CUAIR had 106 members, all of which were major corporations (Cowie 2010: 230–32; Linder 2000: 197–200).

Construction Woes:
Capitalist Neo-Liberalism Takes Shape

The first major battlefield of the capitalist offensive took place in an industry only indirectly affected by globalization. Large industrial capitalists argued that the high costs of construction added to their costs and made them less competitive internationally. However, in terms of the construction industry itself, construction within the U.S. was not subject to global competitiveness. This did not prevent large construction companies from arguing that their ability to compete abroad was damaged by high labour costs. But this argument was patently false as construction companies used cheap and, generally, non-unionized labour in foreign countries (Linden 2000: 196–97).

Construction workers had made tremendous wage gains from 1967 to 1971 through strike actions. Teamsters and west coast longshoremen made similar gains in 1970–71. Auto workers then struggled to make comparable gains. These gains were being made in spite of the existence of the *Taft-Hartley Act* of 1947 and the *Landrum-Griffin Act* of 1959, both intended to undermine unions. *Taft-Hartley* imposed powerful restrictions on unions: it banned workers striking in support of other workers (sympathy strikes), banned unions from refusing to handle goods made by workers on strike (secondary boycott), banned foremen and supervisors from joining a union, required officers to take an oath that they were not Communists and permitted states to pass right-to-work legislation, which banned contracts from requiring that workers belong to a union. The *Landrum-Griffin Act*, while ostensibly focused on union corruption and members' rights, both real issues, was also aimed at all unions. Among other things, the Act strengthened the provisions against secondary boycotts and facilitated management's attempts to influence workers during union organizing campaigns. Nevertheless, this already existing body of anti-union legislation had not proved adequate to stop the spread of militancy among workers.

CUAIR wanted to break the power of unions. One of their main tactics was "double breasting," in which a unionized company set up a second non-union company that would compete for construction contracts. The NLRB decision in 1971 to allow double breasting opened the doors to a tremendous expansion of formally separate companies and placed pressure on unionized companies to compete by forcing concessions from their unionized employees. Smashing construction unions would be the forerunner of the campaign to defeat and intimidate the working class in general, and the specific tactics and strategies developed by CUAIR during this time would go on to be used in other sectors (Rasmus 2006: 135–41).

The success of the corporate offensive against the construction unions was also facilitated by the mid-1970s recession. While the number of construction workers grew by 45 percent from 1965 to 1995 (2,749,000 to 3,993,000), the percentage of workers in unions declined sharply. The major unions in construction were craft unions, such as the carpenters, the boilermakers and the ironworkers. The membership losses of the construction unions were enormous, ranging from 30 to 61 percent (Linder 2000: 385–86). As well, the shift in some unions from rhetorical militancy to grateful servility symbolizes the defeat as well as the compromised character of the labour bureaucracy. As Linder points out, the capitulation of construction unions is well captured in the changing rhetoric of Robert Georgine, head of the Building and Construction Trades Department (BCTD) of the AFL–CIO, who, in 1979, denounced the BRT:

> Georgine, who spoke of a "terrible conspiracy" as early as 1972, accused the Roundtable of seeking the "total annihilation of organized labor." Denouncing the Roundtable's "master strategy," the BCTD issued a special report in 1979 highlighting the union busting activities of the Business Roundtable, which it charged with executing the plan, laid out more than a decade earlier, "to destroy the 17 building trades unions" and "to slash the wages of union carpenters, plumbers and electricians." (Linder 2000: 355)

But over the next three years, the construction unions and Georgine made a sharp retreat, as described by Linder:

> How far unions had backtracked from their outbursts of rhetorical class struggle became clear at a 1982 meeting that explored ways

of halting the decline of union construction. Organized by the AGC [Associated General Contractors of America], the National Conference on Union Construction heard Georgine signal the demise of construction union militancy by conceding that strikes were "the most ridiculous thing that exists on a construction site today," for which there was "absolutely no justification." (Linder 2000: 356)

And by 1985, in a vein that would be repeated by the president of the United Brotherhood of Carpenters in 1998, Georgine expressed his acceptance of the BRT's perspective on unions, which mirrored their acceptance of the concessions demanded by the BRT:

> In 1985 the Roundtable could report to its members that Georgine had told the annual BCTD convention that the U.S. loss of world market dominance, by making construction costs an important economic factor, had "driven owners into the arms of the nonunion contractor." By the 1980s, many of the project's 223 recommendations formed the basis of the working conditions concessions that the construction unions had been forced to yield. (Linder 2000: 357)

And in 1998, speaking to the annual national construction conference of the BRT itself, the president of the carpenters' union, Douglas McCarron, would express his thanks to the BRT:

> The Roundtable's enduring political-economic impact made itself evident at the end of the century in its capacity to shape union leaders' action framework. Attending the Roundtable's annual national construction conference in 1998, the Carpenters' new young president blamed his own and other building trades unions for their decline: "We thought we could be exclusive [and] kept people out of the union, but not out of the trade," said Douglas McCarron, but "[f]air competition drives you to be better [and] there is no doubt that the Business Roundtable put a competitive edge back in the industry." (Linder 2000: 359)

The BRT Emerges

The BRT had been formed by the merger of three powerful corporate groups who already had considerable overlap in their memberships. In 1972, the Labor Law Study Group (LLSG) merged with the CUAIR to form the BRT. The March Group, consisting of the CEOs of forty of the most powerful corporations, joined the BRT the following year (Gross 1995: 234–35). The formation of the BRT was a further political consolidation of the core group leading the big business offensive. The CUAIR, and later, the BRT, using their great wealth, encouraged and financed a huge number of court cases by specific companies to create a thicket of judicial obstacles not only to worker militancy but to the existence of unions themselves.

> The Roundtable project that, in Soutar's view, achieved most was the litigation that it financed to counteract "union power unvarnished." Remaining hidden in the background, the Roundtable funded cases, nominally brought, according to Soutar, by a "poor devil" of a small construction contractor.... The cases, largely dealing with secondary boycott and picketing issues, were designed to establish proemployer precedents that the Roundtable believed could not be expected from a prolabor NLRB or the Congress. (Linder 2000: 211)

The BRT's focus on litigation was very successful — in fact, Douglas Soutar viewed it as its greatest success (Linder 2000: 211). The BRT also moved towards removing the obstacles that Congress, and what it perceived as a pro-labour NLRB, (Gross 1995) posed to its goals of a deep transformation of class relations in the United States. The BRT was effective in its lobbying of both Republican and Democratic presidents as well as congress, whether it was controlled by Republicans or Democrats. Furthermore, the BRT had great success in blocking legislation that would have strengthened unions' and workers' rights (Gross 1995: 236, 239; Phillips-Fein 2009: 198–99).

But while labour reform remained a core area of concern, the BRT had a much wider agenda and deeper hegemonic aspirations. It sought to reshape U.S. culture and laws in general in a pro-business direction (Gross 1995: especially Chapters 11 and 12). Big business, with prodding by neo-conservative writers like Irving Kristol, became more aware that it needed to reshape the common sense of society.

Conservative think-tanks were created or expanded by support from different corporations, foundations and the Business Roundtable. John Post, the executive director of the Business Roundtable, stated: "I can remember the early days [of the American Enterprise Institute], when chief executive officers didn't want to have anything to do with these goddamned professors. Now we understand more about the impact of ideas" (Vogel 1989: 221),

The budget of the American Enterprise Institute (AEI), which had been started in the 1960s, went from $1 million in 1970 to $10.4 million in 1980. In that same period, its staff increased from nineteen to 135 (Vogel 1989: 224).

While the Business Roundtable was the most important class organization of the capitalist offensive that started in the late 1960s, there were a variety of other business organizations that were formed or that grew tremendously in the 1970s. While these organizations promoted a similar economic agenda as the BRT, there were often tensions and conflicts among them on specific issues as well as on strategy. The BRT engaged in discrete but effective lobbying of both political parties and took relatively moderate positions on social policy. The U.S. Chamber of Commerce and the National Federation of Independent Businesses (NFIB), on the other hand, were more conservative than the BRT about a number of issues and hostile to working with Democrats. But on the basic issues of fighting unions and blocking environmental, health and safety legislation, the organizations were united. They were all part of the offensive of the capitalist class, and both the manoeuvres of the top capitalists and the mass mobilization of small and medium capitalists strengthened the political power of capital:

> The Roundtable sought to exercise power by restricting its membership to the biggest of the big companies. The Chamber believed in mobilizing the masses of the business world — any company, no matter how large or small, could join the organization. (Phillips-Fein 2009: 203)

The politicization and mobilization of the business class in the 1970s can be seen in its political turn and organizational growth:

> In 1970 most Fortune 500 companies did not have public affairs officers; ten years later 80% did. In 1971 only 175 companies had registered lobbyists, but by decade's end 650 did, while by 1978 nearly 2,000 corporate trade associations had lobbyists in Washington, D.C. (Phillips-Fein 2009: 188)

Small business had almost no political representation in Washington in the 1960s. The passage of the *Occupation Health and Safety Act* (*OSHA*) and the *Employee Retirement Income Security Act* (*ERISA*) along with the general concern around the social movements of the 1960s made many small businessmen feel threatened and angry — a point reflected by Albert Liebenson, President of the National Small Businesses Association (NSBA):

> In the past, especially on broad economic issues — labor, social security — there was literally no input from small business because none of the associations had the money or the staff.... [But] the more they got hit over the head, the madder they got. (quoted in Vogel 1989: 199)

The membership of the NFIB grew from 300 in 1970 to 600,000 in 1979, while that of the Chamber of Commerce grew from 36,000 in 1967 to 80,000 by 1974. Both organizations dramatically expanded their Washington offices and lobbying activities. The Small Business Legislative Council (SBLC) was formed in 1977 with a membership of twenty trade associations; by 1980 it had grown to include seventy-five national trade associations (Vogel 1989: 199).

The success of these powerful political campaigns (which included both lobbying and mobilizing in the home districts or states of congressmen and senators) was facilitated by changes in the laws controlling the financing of electoral campaigns, which in turn have facilitated a tremendous increase of corporate funding through Political Action Committees (PACs) (Vogel 1989: 206–13; Phillips-Fein 2009: 187–88).

The reshaping of the Democratic Party by big business Democrats towards an even more pro-business direction (Ferguson and Rogers 1986; Selfa 2008) removed the obstacles that Congress (especially when controlled by Democrats) presented in earlier periods to the extreme anti-labour agenda of the BRT and related organizations, obstacles which had led to an initial focus by big business on a judicial and direct action strategy. Now big business could focus on changing the rules of the game by legislative action as well. It took a Democratic president, Bill Clinton, to carry out some of the key proposals of big business:

> The Clinton years of the 1990s symbolized the success of the new order, not the restoration of the old. The end of the Cold War meant that there seemed no longer to be any real alternative to capitalism.... In the frenzy that followed, the CEO and the entrepreneur came to be seen as folk heroes, much as the Business Roundtable had once hoped they might.... The market was the truly democratic sphere, the state for plodding bureaucrats only. The new economic order was one without a place for unions or much role for the government in shaping economic ends. As President, Bill Clinton accomplished much of what Reagan could not: the dismantling of welfare, the deregulation of Wall Street, the expansion of free trade. (Phillips-Fein 2009: 264)

The assault by the CUAIR and the BRT on construction unions was precedent-setting in terms of judicial decisions, corporate strategies and capitalist class organization. Big business, with the Business Roundtable as the key cog, has been tremendously successful in creating more inequality and more job and economic insecurity. The success of the capitalist class in the radical restructuring of the U.S. labour market was facilitated by the weakness of the responses of unions, a weakness not simply rooted in the hope of restoring the *status quo ante* but also rooted in the subordination of the labour movement to the Democratic Party, a party that has generally supported this transformation of the United States in spite of resistance to certain aspects by currents in the party. The Business Roundtable has been successful in making its agenda the parameters of debate and discussion in U.S. society.

Chapter 2

The North American Corporate Offensive

Canada

We are creating a new force ... one that will channel the ideas and talents of Canada's senior business leaders ... our objective is to help strengthen the country's economy, its social fabric, and its democratic institutions. — The Founders 1976, Founding Statement, Business Council on National Issues, Business Council on National Issues, 2001

About CCCE

The Canadian Council of Chief Executives (CCCE) is a not-for-profit, non-partisan organization composed of the CEOs of Canada's leading enterprises. We engage in an active program of public policy research, consultation and advocacy. The CCCE is a source of thoughtful, informed comment from a business point of view on issues of national importance to the economic and social fabric of Canada.

The Council has an outstanding record of achievement in matching entrepreneurial initiative with sound public policy choices. Over the past three decades, the Council has played a private sector leadership role in shaping fiscal, taxation, trade, competition, energy, environmental, education and corporate governance policies. We have been ground breakers in advancing Canada's competitiveness agenda and our work encompasses North American and global issues. We have been referred to as the world's most effective CEO-based organization dedicated to public policy development and solutions.

Our member CEOs and entrepreneurs represent all sectors of the Canadian economy. The companies they lead collectively administer C$4.5 trillion in assets, have annual revenues in excess of C$850 billion, and are responsible for the vast majority of Canada's exports, investment, research and development, and training. (Canadian Council of Chief Executives n.d.)

A Double Threat: Labour Militancy and Interventionist Nationalism

The 1960s and 1970s in Canada were periods of very significant labour mobilization and labour gains, as were the 1960s in the United States. As well, it was a period of intense debate about the direction of national economic policy. Both the labour militancy of the period and the interventionist-nationalist side of the policy debate threatened the ambitions of Canadian capitalists and their U.S. partners. These challenges would lead the most powerful sectors of the Canadian capitalist class to seek a more unified voice to shape public policy and to put workers and unions back in their place. The industrial relations strategy of Canadian capital would go through a major shift from a strategy of consent, concessions and co-optation to one that emphasizes coercion and repression.

The Business Council on National Issues (BCNI) was formed in 1976 as an attempt to give big business a more powerful and cohesive voice in shaping national policy. The BCNI was the idea of two of the most powerful leaders of Canadian business, William Twaits, former CEO of Imperial Oil, and Alfred Powis, President and CEO of Noranda Mines. They explained the council's purpose at a press conference announcing its formation, which was described in the *Board of Trade Journal* of April 1977:

> The press conference was told the purpose of the BCNI is to correct what is seen as a need for a cohesive and responsible business voice on national issues to deal with organized labor and governments that have grown in size as well as propensity to regulate and intervene in the economy. (Davies 1977: 30–31)

The article points out that the new group "includes the greatest collection of heavyweight executive talent in Canada's history" (Davies 1977: 30–31). As the *Board of Trade Journal* said, "[the BCNI's] 91-name membership list ... reads like a Who's Who and covers every major segment of the economy," including Paul Desmarais of Power Corporation, Earle McLaughlin of the Royal Bank of Canada, Paul Leman of Alcan Aluminum, Roy Bennett of Ford and Peter Gordon of Steel Company of Canada, who were all original members (Davies 1977: 30–31).

In the early 1970s, big business was facing significant labour militancy in the context of growing international competition, rising domestic economic nationalism and declining corporate legitimacy in Canada. Big business was also being severely criticized: David Lewis, the leader of the New Democratic Party (NDP), Canada's social democratic party, ran a campaign that was well received by Canadians that attacked "corporate welfare bums" and criticized the heavy subsidies and tax breaks received by business. Twaits and Powis responded to these threats by taking the lead in getting business organized to fight back. They felt that a more united voice was needed by big business to achieve their related goals of enhancing business legitimacy and changing government policy and modelled their new organization, the Business Council on National Issues (BCNI), on the Business Roundtable (BRT) in the United States (Langille 1987: 49).

The BCNI, as did the BRT in the United States, sought to be the quiet but powerful voice of capital in shaping public policy. It sought the development of neo-liberal policies that would restrain labour demands, control inflation and advance the interests of capital. Its composition, as that of the BRT, was impressive. The BCNI's membership is restricted to the CEOs of Canada's top corporations and was initially restricted to the top 150. Today, senior officials of the Canadian Manufacturers' Association (CMA), Canadian Chamber of Commerce (CCC), and Le Conseil du Patronat du Québec (CPQ, Quebec Council of Employers) also participate.

There has been considerable debate over the relative weight of U.S. big business — as compared to various fractions of Canadian big business — both in the formation of the BCNI and in the control of the Canadian economy more generally (Langille 1987). Both Canadian transnational corporations with global ambitions and Canadian branches of U.S. transnationals played a central role in the formation of the BCNI. However, it would be a mistake to see the Canadian capitalist class as predominantly a comprador class (businessmen who act as middle-men between capital from a foreign, imperial power and their home society, such as Canadian executives of a U.S. company in Canada) or a junior partner of U.S. capital (Carroll 2004: 84, 103–4, 124–25).

The control of the Canadian economy by Canadian big business has grown and has become both more concentrated and more transnational in its holdings and perspective in the years since the formation of the BCNI (McBride 2005: 49–58; Carroll and Shaw 2001; Albo 2002), a fact Carroll highlights:

> Foreign control of industry peaked around 1970, just when left-nationalist critics were beginning to label Canada the "world's richest underdeveloped country" (Levitt 1970), and thereafter fell as capitalists in Canada repatriated control of some corporations (with the assistance of nationalist policies in the late 1970s) and some U.S.-based direct investment increasingly went to Europe and the Far East (Dicken 1992: 62–67). (Carroll 2004: 84)

Furthermore, the "centre of gravity [of Canadian capital has] shifted towards interests *based in Canada but operating on a transnational scale*" (Carroll 2004: 85).

Canadian business with global ambitions had and continues to have a perspective that is generally congruent with that of the U.S. multinationals. Canadian capital wanted the U.S. open as a market for their exports, especially natural resources, and a place where they could invest:

> In short, the free trade story really begins not with a "silent surrender" but with the emergence of mature capitalism in Canada. In the lead-up to the free-trade debate, Canadian capital, more concentrated and cohesive than ever, was increasingly interested, like capital elsewhere, in pursuing its own international strategy of foreign direct investment and exports. As well, its organizational capacity was enhanced with the 1975 establishment of the BCNI. (McBride 2005: 51)

Labour Militancy

The relationship between the labour movement and the main social movements was quite different in Canada than in the United States. In the United States, for example, there was a polarization between the mainstream labour movement and the anti-war movement and Black rebellions of the 1960s. While differences and tensions also existed in Canada, there was not the sharp antagonism that existed in the United States. Nor did Canada suffer from the extreme political and ideological domination of its politics by the military-industrial complex or the political subordination of the trade union movement to a capitalist party. These different contexts — less deeply institutionalized racism, less domination by the military-industrial complex and the political links between the labour movement and a social democratic party rather than a bourgeois party — facilitated a different trajectory of labour and social protests in Canada than the United States. As a result, the labour movement was not smashed as early or as fully in Canada as in the United States. The divergent strike experiences of the two countries are indicative of the different timing of the repression of rising worker militancy of the 1960s. Rising workers' militancy in Canada was intertwined with, though at times in conflict with, the electoral successes of the social democratic NDP. These electoral successes led to a brief minority government at the federal level that forced the Liberal Party to make progressive concessions to the NDP. Real gains were made in the mid-1960s: the Canada Pension Plan (CPP) and universal single-payer government medical coverage. Worker militancy outside Quebec, while rooted in its own realities, was stimulated by both the Quebec labour-socialist militancy of the 1960s and the U.S. social movements in the same period.

While the 1960s were a period of great worker militancy in both the United States and Canada, the 1970s saw the beginning of a great divergence of experience. The corporate attack on U.S. unions was already achieving its goals of smashing workers' militancy, whereas Canadian labour militancy continued for a longer period. As Sam Gindin, former assistant to the president of the Canadian Auto Workers (CAW), notes:

> During the sixties, the strike records of Canada and the U.S. were similar. In the seventies, time lost due to strike activity in Canada was almost double that in the U.S. In fact, Canada lost proportionally more days due to strikes than any developed country. (Gindin 1995: 175)

And while increasing state coercion as well as macroeconomic factors dampened and contained militancy, the density of unions grew in Canada, whereas its decline intensified in the United States. And in spite of government efforts, the wave of strikes in Canada continued. As Heron (1996: 94) said, "One quarter of the industrial disputes recorded after 1900 erupted between 1971 and 1975 ... three out of ten strikes in the 1970s were wildcats ... the country was witnessing a full-scale, rank and file revolt."

Sam Gindin offers an explanation for this divergence of experience between the U.S. and Canada:

> In the U.S., the potential of a revival of the union [United Auto Workers] initiated by these young workers was soon lost. The deep recession and the energy crisis in the mid-seventies consolidated that loss and brought discipline back to the workplace. The revolt was essentially over.... Not so in Canada. Although the Canadian social protest movements were relatively weaker, the labour movement was stronger. The defiance of workers lasted longer, and the political influence of labour was actually more powerful in the seventies than in the sixties. In fact, the unions themselves became an important vehicle for placing social issues on the national agenda.... The economic climate in Canada and the deepening of unionization helped to sustain the movement. The Canadian economy benefitted from both the growth in the United States and the devalued Canadian dollar which lowered the costs of exports relative to imports. In the sixties, Canada's workforce grew faster than the workforce in any other major developed country, and unionization kept pace. Workers in manufacturing may have been rebelling against their union leaders, but it was equally clear that the workers wanted to sustain their union. (Gindin 1995: 144)

This growing insubordination was even more dramatic in Quebec, where labour militancy became intertwined with nationalist and socialist politics and a cultural-political renaissance. The Quebec government, fiercely anti-union, had been controlled by an alliance of business, the Catholic Church and reactionary Catholic unions for many years (Jameson 1973: 31–43). The Quebec labour movement went through a major transformation and played an important role in the growing resistance in the 1950s to this repressive provincial regime. The election of a Liberal government in Quebec in 1961 ushered in the "Quiet Revolution," a far-reaching transformation of the province that opened up opportunities for union growth as well as for the expansion of Quebec capital.[1] The transformation involved, among many other political and cultural changes, the growth of a national independence movement. The mainstream proponents of this movement sought an electoral route to independence that would culminate with a referendum to separate from Canada. But there was also a movement, the Front de Libération du Québec (FLQ, Quebec Liberation Front) that believed that armed struggle was the only path to independence. A wing of that movement kidnapped a British diplomat and Quebec's minister of Labour and Immigration, Pierre Laporte. The federal government responded by imposing the *War Measures Act*, which suspended civil liberties and saw almost 500 people arrested and detained. The kidnappings, the strength of the separatist movement and the use of martial law all contributed to a sense of a society in crisis.

The radicalism of the Quebec labour movement developed alongside that of the nationalist movement and also contributed to the sense of crisis among the Canadian capitalist class:

> Quebec union leaders were soon calling for fundamental changes in Quebec society. In 1971 the three Quebec labour organizations [Confederation of National Trade Unions, Quebec Federation of Labour, and the Centrale de l'enseignement du Québec] published the most radical documents seen in North American labour circles in decades; these papers analyzed the exploitation of Quebec workers and made a strong case for a socialist alternative in an independent Quebec. In contrast to social democratic policy statements, these manifestoes emphasized the active role for workers in creating and running a socialist society. (Heron 1996: 104)

And in 1972, the three federations formed a common front and worker militancy exapanded dramatically:

> [They] demanded a uniform wage increase and a common mini-mum wage for the 250,000 workers they represented... and led their membership in the province's first general strike of public-sector workers and the biggest strike in Canadian history.... When the strike leaders, Marcel Pepin, Louis Laberge, and Yvon Charbonneau,

were jailed for defying back-to-work orders, the strike spread spontaneously to large parts of the private sector. In some towns, general strikes erupted, and workers took over radio and television stations. Lacking coordination and effective leadership, the strike petered out within a week. (Heron 1996: 105)

Craig Heron has well described the crisis resulting from the breakdown of the old system of labour control:

> By 1975 the industrial regime that had been laid down in Canada in the 1940s was coming unstuck.... The system of collective bargaining was open enough to encourage unionized workers to try to improve their living standards, but fragmented enough that those improvements would vary widely across the working class and disrupt traditional status relationships between groups of workers, particularly white- and blue-collar employees. The relative weakness of the Canadian state's social welfare provisions also put much pressure on the factory-by-factory negotiations. As the prosperity of the 1950s turned into the economic uncertainty, and especially the spiraling inflation of the 1960s and 1970s, a great turbulence of labour militancy pushed up wage demands and precipitated strikes. Behind the wage demands lay cultural and political challenges that never coalesced into an overt threat to the social order, but were nonetheless disturbing to capitalists and the state. By the early 1970s far too many workers were beyond the control of their bosses, the law, and even their own union leaders, and were demanding concessions that business people and politicians thought were excessive in a healthy capitalist economy. Capitalists and the state were convinced that something had to be done to curb working-class power. (Heron 1996: 105–6)

Capital and the state would strike back. The corporate offensive against workers would gain organizational cohesion with the formation of the BCNI at the beginning of 1976. Its competitiveness agenda — the need to increase managerial powers over workers (now often called "flexibility") and to contain wages and government spending — both of which were blamed for inflationary pressures — was the standard agenda of the corporate offensive in the world beginning in the decade of the 1970s. It would soon become the new consensus among the Canadian political elites and the ideology of this agenda would become hegemonic in later decades.

Interventionist Nationalism

The 1970s were a turbulent economic period in which Canadian capital and Canada's political elites were struggling to find their way. The United States had made a sharp protectionist turn and, as well, the old Keynesian welfare state policies and ideology came under attack by sections of big business, their think-tanks and the corporate mass media. As in the United States, the political elites and virtually all sections of capital shared the view that labour militancy had to be constrained, production costs needed to be reduced and managerial power had to be increased. But the battle over the other key aspects of economic policy within the government bureaucracy, within the long-dominant Liberal Party, and among capitalists themselves continued through the 1970s. All the while, the assault on wages and unions intensified.

President Nixon's protectionist response to the U.S. balance of payments crisis in 1971 threatened to block Canadian exports to the U.S. and shut off U.S. investment in Canada, interrupting the ongoing integration of the two economies. The Canadian government responded by exploring a "Third Option," the diversification of economic relations to lessen dependency on the U.S.:

> Over the ensuing decade the Liberal government introduced many measures aimed at re-establishing federal control over the economy. After decades of treating U.S. firms as good Canadian citizens (an approach that was later known as national treatment), federal policies started discriminating in favour of Canadian capital. Most salient in the mid-1970s were agencies established to screen foreign direct investment (the Foreign Investment Review Agency [FIRA]) and to promote domestic ownership of the Canadian economy (the Canada Development Corporation [CDC]). Then in 1980 came the Liberals' ambitious and notorious National Energy Program (NEP), which was designed to channel economic rents from resources into industrial development. This assertion of authority by the Canadian state over its economic space marked the apogee of its attempt to construct a dominant territorial state and to slow integration — at least at the political level.
>
> Nixonomics and Ottawa's 'Third Option' response interrupted for a decade and a half the steady maturation of an informal Canada–U.S. regime. (Clarkson 2002: 24–25)

But, in the longer run, American protectionism created a great sense of urgency among Canadian business and political elites concerning the need to protect themselves against U.S. protectionism by institutionalizing continental integration (i.e., market and investment access in the United States) in some manner.

While neo-liberalism was becoming the dominant perspective in many capitalist countries, there was resistance to it in Canada lasting through the 1970s. Nixon's actions gave renewed credibility and energy to Canadian economic nationalists. This coincided with growing criticism in Canadian society of the U.S. war in Vietnam and the bitter racial polarization within the United States. Among capitalists, there would be a differentiated and sometimes ambivalent response over nationalism versus continentalism, depending on ideology and sectoral interests.

This division between neo-liberals and interventionist-nationalists was strong within the Liberal Party, the party that dominated Canadian national politics for most of the twentieth century. An openly prominent role of the state in the economy has not been anathema in Canada as it has been in the United States. Canadian capitalist development had long been openly state-linked as part of a nation-building and survival strategy in the shadow of the expansionist United States. As well, the labour movement, a movement that gained strength in the 1970s, was a strong proponent of an interventionist state and was linked to the NDP, one of the two major parties in some provinces and a party that hoped to displace either the Liberals or the Conservatives nationally. The parliamentary system gave the NDP, at times, the leverage of helping to sustain or bring down a minority government. Aspects of the neo-liberal corporate offensive had already been launched by state and capital in the second half of the 1970s, primarily in the form of wage controls and assaults on union and workers' rights. But corporate Canada still faced a strong and resilient labour movement and a widespread state-interventionist and nationalist sentiment. Canadian society and Canadian capital itself had a historical ambivalence on the issue of continentalism versus economic nationalism. For Canada, as in Mexico, a central question in its history was its survival as a nation given its contiguity to the expanding and powerful United States.

Big Business Fights Back

This battle would be bitterly fought out in the 1980s. The 1980s began with the last hurrah of the interventionist-nationalists of the Liberal Party. They were soundly defeated by the power of corporate Canada, which, with the BCNI as its most powerful voice, defeated the last-ditch nationalist thrust. The big business initiative developed a new bipartisan (Liberal-Conservative) consensus around neo-liberalism and continental integration that produced CUFTA, NAFTA and many neo-liberal counter-reforms against the social safety net and state regulation of business.

Canadian and Mexican developments mirrored U.S. developments in many ways. But there were important differences rooted in the structural position of the Canadian and Mexican economies vis-à-vis the U.S. economy.

Both Canada and Mexico were heavily dependent on the U.S. market for their exports, whereas the Canadian and Mexican markets, while significant to some sectors of U.S. capital, were not central to the U.S. economy. This asymmetrical market dependence combined with frequent sectoral protectionism in the United States made Canada and Mexico very vulnerable to U.S. political and policy swings.

The groundwork for the deep integration of Canada into the U.S. economy had been laid by the long history of dependence on exports to the United States and the long presence of U.S. ownership of Canadian companies, a presence fostered by tariffs and other policies that promoted or forced production in Canada for the Canadian market. This strong presence of foreign ownership of Canadian business created a strong mingling of United States and Canadian capital and capitalists within Canada that provided both class/economic networking and social links. While there are important comprador segments, there has also been a growing concentration of capital among Canadian capitalists. We are not talking about a situation of weak, dependent, comprador capitalists in Canada and Mexico. Their leading sectors, such as the Desmarais family of the Power Corporation, are powerful and ambitious (Carroll 2004: 25). They have become actors on the world stage in their own right. They want to control and build "world-class" organizations that will become global leaders (Carroll 2004; McBride 2005).

Access to the U.S. economy was crucial for those sectors of Canadian business that had global ambitions. Fears of U.S. protectionism were based on real experiences and tendencies and became a tool for mobilizing segments of Canadian business that were dependent on exports to the United States. And, in Mexico, the notion that NAFTA would bring forward an avalanche of U.S. investment that would open up markets in Mexico for domestic suppliers and jobs for working Mexicans was central to the selling of free trade to different layers of the bourgeoisie and more generally to the population. The different national histories and regime structures in Mexico and Canada, of course, meant that both the selling of continentalization and the resistance to it would be different. The resistance was much more significant in Canada.

These nationalist responses to Nixon's protectionism were quickly reversed by pressure from the BCNI and the stance of the new government of Ronald Reagan in the United States. The BCNI successfully lobbied against the industrial policy proposed by the nationalist Minister of Industry, Trade and Commerce, Herb Gray, and in favour of an alternate proposal of the Ministry of State for Economic Development. Thomas d'Aquino, president of the BCNI, took some credit for winning this policy battle:

In the words of President Thomas d'Aquino [BCNI] the report "was a good demonstration of what we'd like to see. We'd like to think we helped shape it ... it reflects a lot of the concerns we'd expressed [and] signals a shift in government economic policy in the right direction." (Langille 1987: 58)

This defeat of the last hurrah of Canadian economic nationalism was also reflected in the cabinet shuffle of 1982, in which the more nationalist ministers, including Herb Gray, were replaced by more business-friendly ministers, such as Ed Lumley (Langille 1987: 59; McBride 2005: 58). According to Langille, citing Peter Newman, Marc Lalonde, the new Finance Minister, "went to meet the Business Council executives at d'Aquino's home, where he is alleged to have established a peace pact with the business leaders and to have promised them the government's support." (Langille 1987: 59)

The last foray of Canadian economic nationalism ran up against the realities of the increasingly continental and export-dependent character of Canadian capitalists:

> Faced with a seemingly intractable contradiction between the national mode of its major policy initiatives and an emerging continentally oriented economy in the early 1980s, the government responded by creating the Macdonald Commission. (Inwood 2005: 53)

The formation of the Royal Commission on the Economic Union and Development Prospects for Canada (the Macdonald Commission) in 1982 was an expression of the malaise and conflict over economic policy direction. The cabinet shift and the Macdonald Commission would pave the way for the Liberal-Conservative push into a deeply neo-liberal and continentalist direction. But the consolidation of this new direction towards full-scale integration did not take place until the arrival of the Conservative Mulroney government in 1984, which built on the proposals of the Liberal-led Macdonald Commission:

> In the end, the Liberals asked the Macdonald Royal Commission to resolve the impasse and shut down the 30-year old debate within the techno-bureaucracy on Canada's national policy model. The commission closed ranks around a neoliberal agenda that had mobilized considerable support in the business community and economics profession since the mid-1970s. The commission integrated policy reforms in numerous fields in a coherent discourse of market liberalization and social adjustment that would substantially retrench the federal government's role in the economy and society. With an abiding commitment to market values and incentives, the commis-

sion emphasized the modest administrative-political demands of its package. Politically attractive to a floundering new government seeking to confirm support in the multinational business community and free trade provinces, the Macdonald Commission's neoliberal discourse became the blueprint for two terms of Progressive Conservative government. And since 1993, the Liberals have practiced "Macdonaldism" with a vengeance. (Bradford 1998: 164–65)

The victory of the neo-liberal strategy does not mean, in our view, that the pursuit of a nationalist policy alternative was impossible. Rather, it is to suggest that it would have run into even more overwhelming pressures from the U.S. government, from Canadian and U.S. capital and from some of the provinces. An attempt to resist these pressures would have had to involve a popular anti-business mobilization that would be contradictory to the whole nature of the Liberal Party as Canada's centrist pro-business party. The nature of the Liberal Party and its myriad links to Canadian capital, Canada's export dependence, the increasingly continental-global orientation of big Canadian capital and the global shift towards neo-liberalism all combined to make the continuation of the pursuit of a nationalist direction highly unlikely.

Though the Macdonald Commission did not at first have a clear direction or mandate, it soon found one. The direction did not simply come from the chairman, Donald Macdonald, though his declared "leap of faith" in favour of free trade and his determination and authority played a key role (Inwood 2005: 102).

There had been an increasingly cohesive and organized voice of capital in favour of free trade as a way to consolidate and deepen neo-liberal reforms and protect access to U.S. markets. There was a gradual but decisive shift in the perspective of business towards more bilateral trade and investment integration with the U.S. in the early 1980s. The shift was a result of the business woes produced by the recession of 1982, the strong opposition of business to the interventionist-nationalist initiatives of the federal government and the fear of U.S. protectionism. The BCNI started to make trade with the U.S. a high priority. Thomas d'Aquino spoke of this priority in an interview in 2001, on the twenty-fifth anniversary of the BCNI:

Q. Looking back at the specific contributions that the BCNI has made to the shaping of public policy in Canada, which initiatives stand out most in your mind?

A. The BCNI is probably best known for its campaign during the 1980s in favour of a free trade agreement with the United States. When we first floated the idea early in the decade, no government in Canada favoured outright free trade and there was intense skepticism even in parts of the business community. Massive amounts of homework, extensive consultations and six years of advocacy helped to deliver a wide-ranging deal with our most important trading partner. The Canada–United States Free Trade Agreement proved to be one of the most powerful catalysts for economic and attitudinal reform of this century. This effort would not have been possible without tireless engagement of dozens upon dozens of CEOs who willingly stood up for what they believed was best for Canadian competitiveness, including exports, investment, innovation and job growth. (Business Council on National Issues 2001)

The Canadian Manufacturers' Association (CMA) shifted its position in the first half of the 1980s from its traditional support of protectionism to strong advocacy of free trade. Part of this shift can also be explained by the increased role of imports and exports by Canadian business as world trade became more liberalized. And a large part of the change, as mentioned above, came from the desire of big business to expand on the global stage. A consensus was developing that Canadian business could only prosper if it became more competitive (Doern and Tomlin 1991: 49).

"'Competitiveness' became the central theme of a series of CMA position papers, and papers submitted to the trade policy task force in 1982–83 spoke of 'preferred access' to the U.S. market" (Doern and Tomlin 1991: 48). A trade agreement with the U.S. came to be seen both as a safeguard against U.S. protectionism and a weapon to bring about industrial restructuring in the name of competitiveness. Competitive restructuring meant a less costly, more disciplined and productive labour force. Trade agreements would be a tool in the neo-liberal offensive. The Macdonald Commission made this clear:

> Free trade is the main instrument in this Commission's approach to industrial policy. Our basic international stance complements our domestic stance. We must seek an end to those patterns of government involvement in the economy which may generate disincentives, retard flexibility, and work against the desired allocation of resources. (Macdonald Commission, cited by Bradford 1998: 114)

And, in the words of Gil Winham, one of the key academic architects of the Free Trade proposal of the Macdonald commission, free trade was the first step towards deregulation:

> I concluded that for a trade-dependent country like Canada, because Canada had a much higher trade to GNP ratio than any of these other countries, certainly the United States, that you couldn't deregulate

the economy without free trade, and so therefore free trade becomes a natural sort of notion for deregulating the economy and moving, tilting let us say, because it is always overplayed in the press, but tilting more towards the private market and less towards government interventionism. (Winham, cited by Inwood 2005: 241)

The initiative for a Canada-U.S. free trade agreement came from Canadian business with the BCNI playing the leading role. They started talks with the U.S. officials and U.S. business by the beginning of 1983 as well as with Prime Minister John Turner and the then-leader of the opposition, Brian Mulroney. While at least some U.S. government officials responded positively to the idea of a trade agreement (Doern and Tomlin 1991: 48), U.S. business did not seem terribly interested. Tom D'Aquino, the president of the BCNI, said that "the American government and private sector representatives 'were notably disinterested in the subject in the 1981-1985 period.'" (Langille 1987: 67). Doern and Tomlin, however, saw a more positive response by U.S. government officials to the initiative but also a lack of interest on the part of U.S. big business:

> If U.S. politicians were enthusiastic about a comprehensive trade agreement, American business was not, as BCNI members discovered when they made their first direct test of U.S. business opinion. Shortly after the meeting with [vice-president] Bush [March 1983], BCNI met with its U.S. counterpart, the American Business Roundtable. There they found the American CEOs to be distinctly uninterested in the prospects for a special trade deal. Nevertheless, BCNI continued to press for a comprehensive trade agreement, and for reciprocal trade enhancement. (Doern and Tomlin 1991: 48)

The disinterest of U.S. big business in a trade deal with Canada was not, however, hostility to a deal but, rather, in Doern and Tomlin's view, "simply reflected the usual low profile of Canadian-American issues in the United States" (Doern and Tomlin 1991: 105). The BCNI and the CMA worked on getting more support for a trade deal from business in the U.S. The CMA held a meeting with the National Association of Manufacturers of the U.S. in Washington in April 1987 to discuss these issues. James Robinson of Amex and the Business Roundtable, a "good friend of David Culver, chairman of BCNI and CEO of Alcan," played a key role in the formation of a U.S. business coalition for free trade in July 1987 (Doern and Tomlin 1991: 106). Robinson would go on to play a key role later in the formation of NAFTA, as will be discussed in Chapter 4.

The evolution of Macdonald from state-centred economic nationalist to free trade, neo-liberal continentalist both mirrored and helped shape the evolution of the Canadian capitalist class in that direction. Macdonald was impressed with the breadth of business support for free trade — the BCNI had already been promoting free trade, but now the CMA also supported it and the Canadian Chamber of Commerce did not oppose it. Macdonald himself was immersed in the same circles as other corporate directors: he served on a number of corporate boards (for Canadian companies, American companies in Canada and even some boards of U.S. companies in the United States), and, after leaving politics in 1978, he belonged to the same social clubs and participated in some of the same think-tanks (Inwood 2005: 248–49, 281–82). The importance of the Macdonald Commission was to give bipartisan (Liberal and Conservative) legitimation to the neo-liberal continentalist agenda. The bipartisan character of the neo-liberal agenda is well illustrated by the co-chairmanship of the pro–free trade lobby group the Canadian Alliance for Trade and Job Opportunities, formed in April 1987 by Liberal Donald Macdonald and Conservative Peter Lougheed (a former premier of the oil-rich province of Alberta).

Both the BCNI and the Macdonald Commission saw a free trade agreement as a way to institutionalize neo-liberal policies by international treaty. The free trade agreement was aimed, among other things, as a disciplinary measure aimed at the working class:

> In income security matters, the commission argued for integration of labour market adjustment and social assistance policies. The departure point was that the existing program mix actually contributed to unemployment and expanded welfare caseloads because it was overly generous and insufficiently geared to inducing the unemployed to seek work. Specifically, unemployment insurance required reform on the grounds that benefit levels, eligibility requirements, and regional supports all created disincentives to work. For the same reason, welfare programs, including the family allowance and federal contributions to provincial social assistance payments needed replacement. (Bradford 1998: 115)

The members of the Macdonald Commission were well aware that this would involve a downward harmonization of "Canadian taxation, industrial regulation, and export subsidies much closer to the American pattern" (Bradford 1998: 115).

The BCNI — and an array of other business organizations (the CMA, the Canadian Federation of Independent Business, the Canadian Chamber of Commerce) and think-tanks (the C.D. Howe Institute, the Fraser Institute, the Atlantic Institute for Market Studies) — have been tremendously successful in transforming Canadian discourse and policy to that of neo-liberalism (Carroll and Shaw 2001). Both the BCNI, with strong ties to both the Liberal and Conservative parties, and the Macdonald Commission were crucial in promoting the triumph of neo-liberalism. They both recommended and promoted neo-liberal and continentalist policies that would be carried through by successive Conservative and Liberal governments — from Mulroney (Progressive Conservative) to Chrétien and Martin (Liberal) to Harper (Conservative). Trade agreements were seen as one very important tool for neo-liberal domestic transformation, accompanying ideological efforts to change the climate of public opinion and government policies. As in the United States, this transformation of Canadian society in favour of business did not happen through some impersonal workings of "the market" or processes of "globalization." It was the result of a conscious, organized effort by big business utilizing its vast resources, associated think-tanks and the corporate-owned media. The "talents of Canada's senior business leaders" (founding statement of the BCNI in 1976) have played a crucial role in the neo-liberal, continentalist transformation of North America.

Note

1. As Carroll points out (2004: 103), the rise of Quebec nationalism had a two-fold effect on the composition of the capitalist class in Quebec. On the one hand, important elements of old Anglo-Canadian capital relocated their head offices and/or operations to Toronto and to Calgary. On the other hand, the nationalist provincial governments of Quebec promoted the rise of Quebecois capital. But this neither reflected nor fostered the development of a Quebec national bourgeoisie but rather the expansion of a French-Canadian section of the Canadian bourgeoisie. The French-Canadian bourgeoisie are a major and powerful sector within the Canadian capitalist class and within the BCNI. And, they, like most Canadian capitalists, are continentalist.

Chapter 3

The North American Corporate Offensive
Mexico

We gave the government a deadline to comply with cleaning up of its finances (and) it has fulfilled, even in advance, the verbal promises it made to the business sector and that did not form part of the text of the Pact (1987–88, the Economic Solidarity Pact between government, business and official labor unions), such as the liquidation and (declaration of) bankruptcy of businesses of national significance such as Aeroméxico (major state-owned airline) and Cananea (major state-owned mining company).—Agustín F. Legorreta, then-President of the CCE (Consejo Coordinador Empresarial, Business Co-ordinating Council, former CEO of Banco Nacional de México and active member of the Mexico-U.S. Business Committee) (*UnomásUno*, May 19, 1988, quoted in Valdés Ugalde 1997: 220, translation by authors)

El Consejo Coordinador Empresarial

The Business Council was founded in 1976 as a response of the national productive sector to increasing government intervention in the economy and the application of clearly populist measures.

Our goal is to co-ordinate policies and actions of business organizations, and identify strategic positions with specific solutions that help design policies to boost economic growth and the level of competitiveness of both companies and the country.

As a representative and interlocutor of Mexican businessmen, the CCE works to promote the free market, full democracy, social responsibility and equality of opportunity for people.

Currently, the CCE is composed of seven members (CONCAMIN, CONCANACO, COPARMEX, AMIS, CMHN, CNA Y ABM) and five permanent invitees (CANACO, CANACINTRA, AMIB, COMCE Y ANTAD).

Furthermore, we strengthen our work through collaboration with professional institutions like the Center for Economic Studies of the Private Sector, the Commission on Private Sector Studies for Sustainable Development and the Business Foundation of Mexico. (Consejo Coordinador Empresarial, n.d., translation by authors)

The Post-Revolutionary Regime and Big Business

Mexico recently celebrated the bicentenary of its Revolution of Independence (1810) and the centenary of the Mexican Revolution of 1910–20. The Revolution of Independence, which started as a revolt for political independence, quickly also became an uprising of the lower classes with their own social and economic demands, was defeated — actual political independence came in 1821 as an attempt to maintain the old social regime. And the Mexican Revolution, though having massive participation from peasants and workers, was contained within the path of capitalist development by the militant petty-bourgeois leaders that headed the triumphant currents. Both revolutions have provided a set of revolutionary symbols, language and hopes that have not disappeared from popular consciousness. But the symbols and language that emerged from the revolutionary process came to be incorporated as part of the legitimating ideology of the one-party regime, a regime committed to state-led capitalist development. This regime of state-guided capitalism, which lasted for close to a century, produced an increasingly strong, concentrated Mexican capitalist class, a class that became more and more discontented with the constraints on its political power and the occasional populist flirtations of Mexican governments. Mexican big business, in alliance with foreign capital and international capitalist institutions, has moved Mexico from the path of state-led capitalist development and one-party presidential rule to the path of neo-liberalism and more direct bourgeois rule in the garb of electoral democracy.

The Mexican Revolution was fuelled by discontent over the absence of democracy and the tremendous suffering of the popular sectors — workers, peasants and small business owners — during the *Porfiriato* (1876–1910), as the years of rule by Porfirio Díaz are known. The foreign-dominated economic development that took place had caused great hardship among the popular sectors. There was widespread discontent with the manipulated re-election of Díaz time and again. The discontent boiled over when Díaz, once again, decided to have himself re-elected in 1910. The armed revolt, initiated under the leadership of discontented sectors of the dominant class as well as elements of the middle class, soon took on a more radical character as the popular sectors entered the battle through their own movements (Zapatistas and Villistas) as well as troops for middle-class leaders. The fight within the revolution, a fight that produced a civil war from 1914–17, was also a fight for the support of the popular classes, the fighting forces of the revolution. It pressured the rival leadership, some quite conservative, some radical, to appeal to the popular classes through incorporating social and economic demands into their programs.

The triumphant coalition held a constitutional congress in 1916–17 and adopted a very radical Constitution. It included a labour code, *Article 123*, which specified many rights for workers. It incorporated an article, *Article 27*, that gave the state pre-eminence over land and subsoil rights, which became the basis for much land distribution in the following decades as well as for the nationalization of the oil industry in 1938. These radical and anti-imperialist aspects of the Constitution of 1917 reflected, in part, an attempt by the triumphant leadership to keep popular support as they sought to consolidate their rule (Roman 1976). The power of the new political elite rested on the shoulders of the popular classes as they sought to fight off counter-revolutionary efforts of the large landowners, Mexican and foreign capital and the governments of the U.S., Great Britain, France, Spain and Germany.

The post-revolutionary political leadership based its power on the contained and compartmentalized mobilization of popular forces that could be used to offset the power of the large landowners as well as foreign capital and government. But these leaders were also determined to keep any class from getting strong enough to challenge their rule, a rule that they felt was essential not only for Mexican development as a nation but for its very survival on the border of the expansionist U.S. The U.S. had incorporated half of Mexico's national territory after the Mexican-American war in the mid-nineteenth century. The political leadership that emerged from the Mexican Revolution felt that the very survival of Mexico was at risk from the imperial powers, especially its northern neighbour. They believed that peasants and workers, along with the middle classes, had to develop a strong sense of nationalism and citizenship and this required that Mexico develop with some degree of social justice. While political leaders saw capitalist development as the only possible path of economic development, they believed that the state's role was to guide that development in the national interest. Class struggle, they believed, was an inherent part of capitalism, and the state's role was to develop an equilibrium between classes. No class would be allowed to become predominant.

This ideology was completely congruent with the Bonapartist nature of the new regime, that is, a regime whose power is based on counterbalancing the power of each class or class fraction by other classes or class fractions. It also involves the hypertrophy of the state and the use of populist or nationalist rhetoric to sustain some popular support. The concept is most brilliantly developed in Karl Marx's *The 18th Brumaire of Louis Bonaparte*. The concept of Bonapartism fits the Mexican Revolution very well. The political elite that came to power through the Mexican Revolution of 1910–17 sustained itself by enlarging the state as a source of riches and patronage, playing off different social forces against each other as well as through the use of populist rhetoric and practice. Important sectors of the capitalist class were very opposed to these policies and their occasional unpredictability.

The popular support and legitimacy of the revolutionary regime rested on the promise and practice of major concessions to peasants and workers. These concessions, in turn, gave credibility to the legitimating ideology of revolutionary nationalism. The political elite sought national capitalist development with social justice, and were determined to keep both foreign and domestic capital from dominating the state. "Revolutionary nationalism" was their program, a perspective in which the state would promote capitalist and non-capitalist development in a framework where the state would be the conciliator of the inevitable class conflicts. At the same time, they sought to keep the popular classes divided so that they could not challenge the post-revolutionary elite.

There was a wide spectrum of views within the political elite as to the right mix between social justice and capitalist development, but, in general, there was a shared belief that a national capitalist route of development was the only viable path. Even those who were socialists, with few exceptions, felt that Mexico had to develop through capitalism. But there was also the widely shared belief that the excesses of capitalism could be contained by an actively interventionist state, that a balance between different class interests could be maintained for the sake of the broader national interest. Capitalist development also provided opportunities for members of the political elite to advance their private interests and to become capitalists themselves.

Though there were important differences between the various Mexican presidential regimes of the Partido Revolucionario Institucional (PRI, Institutional Revolutionary Party) in its seventy-plus years of rule, a constant was the pursuit of national capitalist development. The extent and the character of concessions made to workers and peasants varied from president to president, reaching their peak in the presidency of Lázaro Cárdenas (1934–40), when major land redistribution was carried out, the foreign owned oil industry was nationalized and separate worker and peasant organization was promoted. However, the turn to the right in the last period of the Cárdenas presidency, a turn culminating in the selection of Manuel Ávila Camacho to be the next president, set Mexico on a developmental path in which there would be much more repression and much fewer concessions to the popular classes. From 1940 on, with few exceptions, the policy of successive Mexican governments was capitalist development at any price. Trade union independence, already seriously undermined by the incorporation of unions into the ruling party as well as by repression, became even more constrained and limited to very few unions. Trade unions almost completely became instruments for the political advancement of their leaders and for government control over the working class. Corruption and strong-arm methods of control of unions and workers were accompanied by gains in the social wage (health and housing benefits) for important sectors of the unionized working class. Though there were recurrent rank-and-file rebellions, union democracy and independence were definitively smashed and *charrismo* (specifically Mexican term for state-linked, authoritarian and often corrupt union oligarchies),[1] old or newly imposed, was consolidated.

Mexico's rapid economic growth in the post-World War II period, the so-called "Mexican Miracle" (1940–68), has generally been attributed to its ISI (import substitution industrialization) strategy, in which the state promoted the development of nascent national industry through tariffs and other regulations. This strategy was not unique to Mexico. Similar processes had already occurred in other cases of late industrialization in the first half of the twentieth century, as in southern Europe. But the distinctive character- istic of Mexico (and with variations, of Argentina and Brazil) was the tight control that the Mexican state was able to develop over the working class. Cheap wages and labour discipline was not the only important subsidy that the Mexican state granted to the nascent bourgeoisie. But it was the most important.

Strong state regulation, combined with the presence of an enormous peasantry, a supplier of a plentiful reserve army of labour for the incipient industrial zones, shaped the basic framework for this process of capitalist development. The state also nurtured infant industries by granting them cheap inputs through the state's discretional use of Mexico's abundant re- sources. The state assured cheap and well-controlled labour to small, medium and large capitalists through the use of *charro* unions and, when necessary, violence. The government's power to promote profits for specific private capitalists added to its great power over Mexican business.

Though the economic power and political influence of Mexican big business grew significantly in the period of the "Mexican Miracle," the regime kept business at the margins of political power. The ruling party- state elite sought to keep its relative autonomy. It acted to preclude direct domination by the big business class and was willing to come down heavy on any direct challenges. Discrete, private discussions were fine; open criticism of the government was not. Thus, while the political elite was constrained by the nature of its goal of capitalist development as well as the strength of some sectors of capital, it also had important leverage that it could use against individual capitalists or sectors of capital. As well as imposing costs and obstacles on difficult companies, the political elite could and did even expropriate some businesses. The occasional use of these levers against "selfish" capitalists would not only give a strong message to other capitalists, but also contributed to the legitimation of the regime as a "revolutionary nationalist" one. Popular sectors could be mobilized as part of this disciplining and legitimating process. The state also actively sought to keep the business class divided, a policy it also carried out among the popular sectors. As well, most sectors of Mexican business did very well in this ISI period, aided by government policies and subsidies and this profitable relationship with the state limited the more extreme anti-regime views within the capitalist class to a minority.

Big business, however, while kept away from direct political power, had significant power based on its wealth and control of key sectors of the economy. Capitalists, acting individually or in a co-ordinated manner, have powerful economic levers that any government has to take into account in shaping policy. Capital flight, the withholding of investment and the reloca-tion of plants are all potent weapons that can impose powerful constraints or penalties on a government and on its ability to carry out its programs, or even survive.

Beyond opposition to specific governmental policies, business's big fear was that the great degree of state autonomy, the revolutionary rhetoric of the regime and the demands of workers and peasants could, as it at times did, lead to major attacks against specific capitalist interests or the interests of capital as a whole. Big business was kept distant from governmental power at the same time that governmental policies generally favoured the interests of big business. Sections of big business, especially the northern business elite, centred in Monterrey, persistently and bitterly opposed the strong, relatively autonomous state but co-operated with it in their quest for riches.

The Transition: The Struggle for Hegemony

The long-standing tensions between the political elites and the Mexican bourgeoisie would come to a head during the presidencies of Luis Echeverría (1970–76) and José Lopez Portillo (1976–82) as the government tried to deal with various political and economic crises in ways that deeply disturbed busi-ness (Hellman 1983: 196–209). Echeverría had been secretary of government (interior) during the presidency of Gustavo Díaz Ordaz (1964–70), when a mass student movement developed in late July 1968 protesting government abuses and political repression. These protests were joined by thousands of ordinary citizens and were seen to be especially threatening as they followed student and worker revolts that same year in France, Czechoslovakia and elsewhere that had threatened existing governments. As well, Mexico was preparing to host the 1968 Olympics and showcase itself as a modern, stable and progressive nation. Hundreds of thousands of students and ordinary citizens participated peacefully in the protests that started at the end of July and continued through the period leading up to the 1968 Summer Olympics. The government was determined to end the protests, and on October 2, the military carried out the infamous Tlatelolco massacre, opening fire on a peaceful gathering of protestors. It is not possible to know how many people were killed and wounded as many of the bodies were quickly removed by the government. Researchers now generally agree that around 300 people were killed, while acknowledging that solid data is not available (National Security Archive, George Washington University 2006). Hundreds more were wounded, and around 2000 were arrested (Stevens 1974: 232–37; Hellman 1983: 173–86; Poniatowska 1975). As secretary of government, Echeverría, along with the president, was blamed for the massacre. When Echeverría became president in 1970, he sought to regain both his legitimacy and that of the regime by political liberalization, which opened up channels of dissent, and by populist policies of wage increases, land reform and economic nationalism. He put forward policies that reaffirmed governmental control over foreign investment but, at the same time, tried to put pressure on Mexican capitalists to modernize by cutting back on subsidies and tariffs.

The government feared that the militancy of the mass student protests of the late 1960s would spread to the working class. The government also wanted to renew hope that change could happen within the system as a number of students, teachers and other citizens had turned to guerrilla struggle after 1968. Echeverría's changes in the regime's strategy — as well as the rise of worker struggles — disrupted the fragile equilibrium between the state elite, big national capital and the multinationals that had developed during the period of *desarrollo estabilizador* (stabilized development). As well, Echeverría sought to pressure business to become more competitive by withdrawing some government subsidies. Business felt threatened by Echeverría's flirtation with economic nationalism and populism and the rise of workers militancy, which showed prospects of spilling beyond the terrain of narrowly economic interests.

The sharp rise in business discontent in response to Echeverría's flirtation with populism and the growth of labour militancy in the early 1970s led to the formation of the Consejo Coordinador Empresarial (CCE) in 1975. It was the umbrella organization of business and sought to bring together the varied and often discordant voices of business. The CCE included seven national associations representing all sectors of Mexican business. The key force in the formation of the CCE was the Consejo Mexicana de Hombres de Negocios (CMHN, Mexican Businessmen's Council). The CMHN had been formed in 1962 by twelve of the most powerful businessmen in Mexico, who sought to strengthen business influence by forming this highly exclusive and secretive organization, which had the goal of discretely lobbying and pressuring the government. The CMHN, which now has forty-two members, continues to be the most powerful group within the CCE as well as the most powerful business group in Mexico. It has provided most of the funding for the CCE and many of the presidents of the CCE came from the CMHN (Cypher and Delgado

Wise 2010; Puga 2004; Schneider 2002). The CCE itself was structured in a non-democratic manner, with each of its member associations having one vote. The handful of members of the CMHN, therefore, had the same formal voting power within the CCE as did CONCANACO (Confederación de Cámaras Nacionales de Comercio, Confederation of the National Chambers of Commerce), which had 500,000 affiliates.

There were differences among the member associations of the CCE on issues of trade policy as well as the type of relationship that business should have with the government. The CCE became the arena in which business sought to develop a unified voice and, if not, to neutralize dissident voices, such as CANACINTRA (Consejo Nacional de la Industria de la Transformación, National Chamber of Manufacturing Industries). CANACINTRA was not itself a member of the CCE as it was a section of a larger organization, CONCAMIN (Confederación de Consejos de Industria, Confederation of Chambers of Industry). CANACINTRA represented small and medium businesses, most of whom had developed in the ISI period and relied on the domestic market, protectionist policies and state subsidies. CANACINTRA feared the impact of free trade, but the more powerful organizations of the CCE, such as the CMHN, COPARMEX (Confederación Patronal de la República Mexicana, Mexican Employers' Association) and ANIERM (Asociación Nacional de Importadores y Exportadores de la República Mexicana, National Association of Importers and Exporters) strongly supported free trade, while CONCANACO and CON-CAMIN only leaned towards free trade. The battle within the business class was dominated by the largest businesses and richest men in Mexico in alliance with transnational, mainly American, corporate allies.

Business — as well as conservative elements in his party — sought to destabilize the Echeverría regime by provoking unrest in order to make the government look incompetent. Echeverría retreated under their pressure. He backed down from his populist and reformist program by 1973 and offered significant concessions to business (Hellman 1983: 205–6). The power of business was further strengthened by the financial and economic crisis of 1976 that forced Mexico to go to the International Monetary Fund (IMF) for help. The leverage of the IMF strengthened the hands of big business and their allies within the government. Thus, the conservative forces in Mexican society, with the aid of international capital and the IMF, were able to pressure the government to back down from its populist leanings.

The new government of President José López Portillo sought to restore business confidence and reassure the IMF. Business-state relations warmed when López Portillo made conciliatory gestures to business in the first years of his presidency. The moderate forces in business were strengthened and business retreated from direct policy criticism. The government subsidized profits through the provision of loans below the rate of inflation and of inputs from the vast state sector (oil, other raw materials, rail transport) below their real costs of production. López Portillo's government was able to do this by massive borrowing based on the hoped-for revenues from the discovery of vast new oil reserves. However, oil revenues failed to rise as expected, and borrowing rates were very high. While these policies greatly enriched the wealthy and powerful, they sowed the seeds of Mexico's financial crisis. Mexico's debt crisis both saddled the Mexican people with astronomical public indebtedness and increased the leverage of foreign capital.

Mexico's economic crisis peaked towards the end of López Portillo's presidency as the country faced massive capital flight, the possible bankruptcy of the state and the financial panic of August 1982. The peso was radically devalued and prices on key consumer goods — gasoline and electricity — skyrocketed; Mexico was near economic collapse and there was a deepening crisis of political legitimacy. The President, with only months remaining in his term, responded by announcing the nationalization of the banks on September 1, 1982, as a strategy to try to gain control over the economic free fall (Marois 2008; Cypher 1990: 120–21). The Mexican government needed to assure foreign creditors that their debts would be paid so as to keep lines of credit open. The manner in which the nationalization was carried out shocked big business as there was no forewarning or consultations. The act of nationalization against one of the most important fractions of business, the banking sector, showed the continuing capacity of government to move against sections of business. And the President dressed his action in the rhetoric of revolutionary nationalism to mobilize popular support and restore the declining legitimacy of the regime.

Big business did not respond in a uniform way to the nationalization. Business opposition to the nationalization was widespread, with the exception of some industrial capitalists who had bad experiences with the banks. But there were important strategic differences in the responses of business. The more radical wings of the business sector, such as COPARMEX, and the ex-bankers called, without success, for a general strike by business. More moderate elements felt, quite correctly, that quiet lobbying with the incoming president, Miguel de la Madrid, would be more effective in reversing the nationalization (Cypher 1990: 120–26).

Business became more united on the need to transform the relationship between capital and the state. The surprise nationalization showed the capacity of the state to act with tremendous autonomy. Business, while still divided over competing company or sectoral interests as well as political differences, would unite around curbing the autonomy of the state. Business would set the boundaries of state activity.

A consensus emerged that the regime itself had to be changed: "Business now had a longer time horizon and its goals were more political and less narrowly instrumental" (Thacker 2000: 107). Business now had hegemonic aspirations though, of course, there were still important policy divisions within business on the role of the state in the economy and on free trade. The most powerful sectors of business were in favour of a diminished economic role of the state, the destruction of unions and an opening of the economy to foreign capital. These sections of business would be strengthened by the massive privatization of the 1980s and 1990s and would be joined by powerful new sectors created by these very privatization projects. At the same time, those business sectors tied to the domestic market, state subsidies and state protection from external competition would be severely weakened.

López Portillo's nationalization of the banks occurred at the very tail end of his presidency. The incoming president, Miguel de la Madrid (1982–88), was not even consulted. The presidency of de la Madrid can be seen as a transitional presidency to the neo-liberal triumph. He first sought to restore business confidence while maintaining the pre-eminent role of the state in guiding the economy. But business was not satisfied with this approach and fought hard during the early years of his presidency to shift policy and power more to the neo-liberal right, to change tripartite consultations (business, unions and the state) to bipartite (business and the state) and to insulate the government from populist temptations.

President de la Madrid sought to rebuild business confidence and support for the government. He took the dramatic step of restoring the wealth and financial power of the ex-bankers and carried out other policies to promote wealth accumulation of old and new sections of business even while the economy suffered. These measures greatly strengthened the power of big business and affected the internal make-up of the business class:

> The process of restoring the financial elite was complex. But, in essence, it was reducible to the following: First, compensation was paid for all nationalized property; second, the ex-bankers could own up to 34 percent of the stock of the nationalized banks and could function as managers on the boards of directorship of the public banks; and third, the ex-bankers could buy back from the government all nationalized property, except the *deposit* banks. In effect, the *investment* banks (known as "non-bank financial intermediaries") were again taken over by the financiers of Mexico. Finally, and most importantly, the stock exchange became the vehicle by which the government sought funding for the internal debt. With payments on the internal debt (annual interest) amounting to as much as that paid on the external debt, the operators of the stock exchange were able to capture an extremely lucrative underwriting business. (Cypher 1990: 163)

The other major policy aimed at gaining business confidence and consolidating Mexico's neo-liberal path was massive privatization. The public sector included much more than services: it was very important in natural resource extraction (oil and mining) as well as manufacturing, as the government set up companies to subsidize cheap inputs for private capitalist development or to remove bottlenecks that were either not profitable or were beyond the scope of Mexican private capital. These public companies had been established to facilitate the state-guided private capitalist project. As of 1987, public firms provided 41.2 percent of government income, 3.3 times more than income tax, and were the second source of government revenue. (Cypher 1990: 127). These companies included Pemex (the national oil company, which has a monopoly on production and distribution), Fertimex (a fertilizer monopoly), Telmex (the national telephone company), CONASUPO (a national food distributor with retail outlets throughout the country), the two national airlines, Aeroméxico and Mexicana, and Mexico's national railways (Cypher: 128). The number of state-owned enterprises decreased from more than 1100 in 1982 to slightly more than 200 in 1994, with the vast majority of the privatizations taking place during the Salinas presidency (1988–94). Pemex was partially privatized by stealth, as different functions involved in the petrochemical industry were redefined as non-essential and contracted out to private companies. Carlos Slim, now the richest man in the world, became the main owner of the privatized telephone monopoly (Forbes Magazine, n.d.). The acquisition of the giant Cananea copper mines gave Jorge Larrea and his Grupo Industrial Minera México control of 96 percent of all copper production in México (Concheiro Bórquez 1996: 88). The privatizations were done behind closed doors with the government selecting potential bidders. The "restoring [of] the financial elite" (Cypher 1990: 163) and the massive sell-off of government companies at bargain prices "fortified the development of the new, independent, financially connected entrepreneurial class" (Thacker 2000: 116). The wealth and power of big business increased, as did the concentration of capital in Mexican society and within the business class (Concheiro Bórquez 1996: 87–107).

The neo-liberal assault on the state sector faced strong opposition from the political-economic elite that sat in the commanding positions in that sector. Their power and privileges were rooted in state enterprise as well as their simultaneous or sequential roles in the ruling party or government bureaucracy. Their state-based positions required the continuation of a powerful state economic sector; the ideology of revolutionary nationalism and the directing role of the state within a capitalist economy fit their interests well. As well, the *charros* sitting atop the large unions in the public sector, who were also intertwined with the ruling party and the state, shared the same ideology and interest in a strong public economic sector as the state elite. And workers in this sector often had better jobs and benefits than those in the private sector. As well, important sections of small and middle-sized capital depended on state support and took a positive position towards the government's role in the economy, at least until the late 1970s.

The debate within the government and the ruling party over economic policy was rooted in rival political, cultural and economic projects. The top Mexican capitalists, in alliance with their foreign allies, moved to implement a neo-liberal agenda of an export-oriented, open economy and a state that would eliminate the social wage while increasing the state's coercive power. But, along with a different economic direction, the new power bloc — with powerful help from the private owners of the major media — promoted an economic-cultural model that sought to institutionalize a culture of possessive individualism and destroy the remnants of Mexico's communalist cultures, communalist cultures that had been given a partial reprieve by the Mexican Revolution and subsequent decades of revolutionary nationalist hegemony.

Massive privatization destroyed the power base of key sectors of the state elite while creating great wealth and power for new and old sectors of capital. Some of the elites and bureaucrats of state enterprises were able to find soft landings by transferring their skills and energies to the private sector. Others experienced downward mobility. Some of the *charros* were able to keep control of their reduced membership and have sought to sell their services of labour control to the new private owners. But very few workers in the formerly public transportation and industrial sectors found soft landings. The massive elimination of public companies, the degradation of working conditions and the destruction of collective agreements at those companies that were privatized, as well as the failure to produce new jobs in the regions where state enterprises had been located, have all contributed to the hard landing of most of the former workers in the state sectors. It is the residue of this old historic bloc, both its elite members and its mass base, that continue to provide major support for the revival of the modernized revolutionary nationalism of Andrés Manuel López Obrador or for the return of the PRI to the presidency, wishfully hoping that such a change would mean the return of at least some aspects of the economic benefits of the old regime.

The Neo-Liberal Regime: Bourgeois Domination Without the Consolidation of a Hegemonic Historic Bloc

Mexico's one-party system, the major role of the state in the economy and the rhetoric of revolutionary nationalism obscured the tremendous power that business had been developing as well as its role in bringing about the neo-liberal regime and competitive elections. The expanded power of business would combine with a series of economic and political crises to transform the balance of forces within Mexico. The increasingly direct political role of sections of business, mostly through the right-wing Partido Acción Nacional (PAN, National Action Party), led the PRI to seek to give business a more direct presence in the PRI and in the state apparatus. As a result, the PRI began to run business candidates against the PAN's business candidates, more business people were recruited to work within the state and the more pro-business departments of the state gained power over the more traditionally nationalist departments. The transformation of the state from a Bonapartist capitalist state towards more direct capitalist domination was well underway in the 1980s and would be intensified in the 1990s. In 2000, the first victory of an opposition presidential candidate, the former President of Coca Cola Mexico, Vicente Fox of the PAN, over the ruling party's candidate was a milestone in the legitimation and triumph of the power of big business, albeit in the garb of a "democratic transition." On June 21, 2001, President Fox (2000–6) described his government as a "government of entrepreneurs, by entrepreneurs and for entrepreneurs" (Rodriguez 2001). The very real electoral space and democratic dynamics that were opened up were subordinated to the dynamic of the rise of more direct capitalist rule and increased repression by the state and private forces. The concentration of wealth and power through privatization and other government policies intensified the domination by big business and both constrained and hollowed-out the processes of democratization.

The corporate offensive was the main driving force in the neo-liberal transformation of Mexico, as it was in the United States and Canada. But, in Mexico, the corporate power bloc had to change the political order and aspects of the political culture in order to achieve its hegemonic aspirations and bring about its desired policy changes. Big business was joined in these goals by sections of the political elite, who had moved away from Keynesian and statist ideas, and by the influence and pressures from international actors promoting neo-liberalism and free trade. The growth of the influence of neo-liberal economics and its impact on Mexican government technocrats studying in the United States as well as the leverage exerted by the IMF and the United States during various Mexican crises was, of course, crucial in leading to the triumph of the neo-liberal corporate offensive already underway in Mexico. But it is mistaken to see Mexico's turn to neo-liberalism and free trade as simply a result of these external factors, and the emphasis on these external factors obscures the struggle for hegemony within Mexico. Capital has great structural and instrumental power at its disposal even when the state has a great degree of autonomy. Capital flight, whether carried out to protect one's wealth or as a deliberate strategy of pressure, can produce economic crises that undermine government support. And the great wealth and power of big business allows them to lobby even within the labyrinth of a one-party regime. These direct and indirect forms of capitalist power have, at times, been decisive in shaping governmental policy.

The restiveness of Mexican capital under Bonapartist capitalist development changed into hegemonic aspirations. The Mexican capitalist class had to transform the relationship between capital and the state in order to achieve its policy goals. As described above, the political elite that controlled the state had a great deal more autonomy than did the political elites of the United States and Canada while the domestic bourgeoisie had much less structural or political power over state elites in Mexico. The interpenetration of the capitalist class with the state was much more limited in Mexico than in the rest of North America until recent decades. The ideology of the regime was "revolutionary nationalism," an ideology that posited the leading role of the state not only in economic development but also in maintaining equilibrium between capital and labour. The big bourgeoisie was kept outside the official party in the one-party state, while labour and peasant organizations composed two of the three official sectors. The fractious ideological conflicts and differences in sectional economic interests within the capitalist class were utilized as part of the government's strategy for keeping the Mexican bourgeoisie in its place in the economic sphere and outside of politics. Business could not completely overcome its internal divisions over ideology, strategy and tactics or different policy interests (especially over trade and protection), but over time, a dominant if not completely ideologically hegemonic fraction, came to ascendancy within the business class, an ascendancy strongly helped by government policies and favouritism in the process of privatization. But big business had also to fight for the legitimacy of business playing any political role whatsoever.

Cristina Puga has described three stages in the transformation of state-capital relations and economic policy in Mexico. The period from 1945–85 was protectionist in policy; business was organized in an obligatory corporatist manner, and the discourse of business varied from following the official line of the regime to confrontational, depending on the sector or business association and the particular conjuncture. Puga depicts 1985–93 as a transitional stage where capital's key relationship with the state is through *concertación* (tri-partite pacts) and the rise of representation of capital by voluntary organizations of the capitalist class, headed by its most powerful members. The third stage, from 1994 to the present, which she calls "globalization," involves an increasing role of the top capitalists in forging state policy in an integrated manner with top state officials. The discourse is one of "co-responsibility." The new scheme of co-ordination between business and the state "also implies a gradual blurring of boundaries between entrepreneurial activity and governmental activity that, although they are kept as two distinct domains with differentiated responsibilities, they are interwoven in numerous spaces" (Puga 2004: 64, translation by authors).

While big business has been able to reshape the state and public policy, it has not achieved ideological hegemony over the overwhelming majority of the popular classes for two main reasons. First of all, big business and the rival political party elites have been unable to develop an electoral process that could legitimate the political regime. In 1988, the unexpected emergence of a third, populist and nationalist electoral force in the candidacy of Cuauhtémoc Cárdenas through the Frente Democrático Nacional (FDN, National Democratic Front), later to become the Partido de la Revolución Democrática (PRD, Party of the Democratic Revolution) in 1989, disrupted the hopes of the bourgeoisie and political elites for the establishment of electoral alternation between the right-wing business party, the PAN and the old state party, the PRI, which was now neo-liberal. Cárdenas won the election, but the PRI stole it, which led to massive protests. And once again, in the presidential elections of 2006, the party of the right, the PAN, stole the presidential elections from Andrés Manuel López Obrador and the PRD, again leading to massive protests. Though electoral hopes persist among broad sectors of the population, the frauds of 1988 and 2006 as well as the manipulations in the 2012 election linger in popular memory. The smell of fraud that existed during one-party rule has now continued in the so-called democratic transition, the change from one-party rule to multi-party electoral competition.

Secondly, the regime's neo-liberal policies have been devastating to the lives of the popular classes. These neo-liberal policies have produced wide-scale and persistent, albeit fragmented, resistance from social, community, labour and indigenous movements throughout Mexico. The struggles of the popular social movements have deepened and widened the awareness of the linkages between neo-liberalism and the hollowed-out "democratic transition." This "democratic transition" has come packaged with a devastating attack on the lives of ordinary people. The combination of the continuing fraudulent electoral processes, the relentless devastation of living standards and the persistent popular protests have produced an increasingly militarized repressive state and a sullen, but potentially explosive, discontented populace. Mexico's present and historical volatility, in sharp contrast to the situation in the United States and Canada, where capitalist domination has been very secure, has been a special concern to both Mexican and U.S. capital.

Note

1.   The term *charrazo* was used to describe a coup by the state and some opportunistic leaders in the railway workers union against the elected leadership of the union in 1948. It has become a general term in Mexico to describe corrupt,

undemocratic union leaders and practices. A *charro* refers to a leader and *charrismo* to the practice of state-linked, corrupt, undemocratic unions. The term derives from the highly stylized horsemen's attire worn by the imposed leader. It is now a term of opprobrium often chanted in labour demonstrations. There is a range of *charro* unions and practices in terms of the degree to which, for whatever purposes, they seek to defend workers and collective agreements and the degree to which they simply seek to sell control. While once an integral part of the ruling party in a one-party regime, they now can best be described as regime-linked, working with whichever of the two neo-liberal parties are in power and are trying to maneuver within the rivalry between these parties to better leverage their bargaining power in terms of preserving their control of their unions.

Chapter 4

The North American Corporate Offensive
NAFTA

We promoted an exciting, powerful, novel idea — that the private sector has the power to provoke change. Through our ideas and our capital, we could influence public policy, economies and people's well being. Imagine our excitement when President Miguel de la Madrid, and subsequently President Carlos Salinas de Gortari, not only believed in the concept but openly espoused it for the future of Mexico. — Rodman C. Rockefeller, long time co-chair of MEXUS (Mexican–U.S. Business Committee) discussing the work of the committee in his acceptance speech upon receiving the Orden Mexicana del Águila Aztec (Order of the Mexican Eagle) from Mexican President Ernesto Zedillo in 1996, quoted in Christian Kelleher, 2006–7.

While business and the state in Mexico were developing their rapprochement in the 1980s, both sought to open the country to more foreign investment. They were joined in these efforts by U.S. big business that also had long wanted to make Mexico a more "open" economy with greater investment security. The 1982 bank nationalization in Mexico had not only galvanized the Mexican bourgeoisie to play a more unified and aggressive role but also activated the embryonic alliance between the Mexican and U.S. bourgeoisie. The broad ideological conceptions of capitalist statesmen in "open economies" and "free markets" often diverge, if not conflict, with specific interests of capitalists in protecting their national markets for themselves. While sectors of the U.S. bourgeoisie used Mexico's recurrent economic crises to bargain for a greater or faster opening for U.S. interests, Mexico's great groups of oligopolic power fought successfully to preserve their state-protected markets. NAFTA did not preclude Mexican legislation from retaining the powerful entry barriers for foreign corporations in the realms of telecommunications (Telmex), television (Televisa and TV Azteca) and, in a certain sense, publicly contracted construction (ICA, Mexico's giant construction company). Other groups, such as grain growers, only received a delay in implementation of free trade for ten years. Ownership of the banking system by Mexican capitalists was destroyed in the economic crisis of 1995, and ownership of the major banks is now completely in the hands of foreign capitalists — BBVA and Banco Santander (Spain), Citibank (U.S.) and HSBC (Great Britain) (Curzio 1998: 206). These specific tensions and conflicts of interest, however, are housed within the overall hegemonic project of neo-liberal transformation and continental integration, a shared project of U.S. and Mexican capital. Neo-liberal continental integration was not forced on the leading sections of Méxican capital.

The negotiations over NAFTA and its promotion in the U.S. brought the leading sectors of big business in the U.S. and Mexico closer together. In Mexico, in fact, as discussed in Chapter 3, it was also a process in which the coming together of state and capital in a common project was deepened. While a direct role of big business in government is relatively new in Mexico, it is old hat in the United States and Canada. The seeds of NAFTA had been planted in U.S. soil by big business and Republican presidents and were brought to fruition by a Democratic president. For James Robinson, former head of Amex and member of the Business Roundtable's task force on trade, President Bill Clinton was the hero in the battle for NAFTA. In an interview with John R. MacArthur, he expressed his admiration for Clinton's role: "NAFTA happened because of the drive Bill Clinton gave it.... He stood up against his two prime constituents, labour and environment, to drive it home over their dead bodies" (MacArthur 2000: 275).

But while Clinton played a major role in the passage of NAFTA, there were many other "heroes" of the campaign for NAFTA in the United States, including the many CEOs of the BRT, members of the Mexico–U.S. Business Committee (MEXUS), Democratic Party leaders (outstanding were William Daley, Rahm Emanuel and Mickey Kantor) as well as prominent Republicans, such as Ronald Reagan and George H.W. Bush. The Mexican government also played a "heroic" role by investing $25 to $50 million within the United States to sell NAFTA.

NAFTA was developed by a transnational business and government alliance. It was sold to legislative bodies and, to different degrees, to the public by that transnational business and government alliance. It was big business in Mexico and the United States, in collaboration with important state actors, that was the moving force for the development of NAFTA, as it was big business, along with key state actors in Canada and the United States, who pushed through CUFTA. That the big capitalists of these countries played the central role in these processes is not to deny the crucial importance of political actors. The state and big business in a capitalist society do operate in different domains and have formally separate institutional configurations. But they are intertwined through shared ideology, think-tanks, the movement of personnel between the two realms, advisory bodies, political parties, lobbying organizations and conferences, such as the Davos World Economic

Forum (WEF). The dynamics of capitalism and the purposeful efforts of the capitalist class both push the state in certain directions and set boundaries on alternatives. There are many conflicts, of course, within these boundaries, as there are divergent and conflicting interests and ideologies among capitalists and within society more generally. The capitalist state is an inseparably intertwined institutional complex of the economy and the political order. The two domains do not simply condition one another; they are interwoven with one another. Ignoring one or the other or treating them as if they are historically and empirically independent only mystifies our understanding of our political economic pathways.

CUFTA and NAFTA cannot be understood without dealing with the major role of big business in creating the ideological framework for free trade agreements and promoting them through the various means made possible by their power and wealth. Ignoring the role of peak business organizations — or treating business as simply one of a variety of influences from civil society — misses the centrality of their role and mystifies the processes. As will be seen below, the capitalist class plays a decisive role in shaping the direction of capitalist society. Though other groups have influence in a politically democratic society, their influence is much more limited. When the capitalist class develops relative unity and a broadly common hegemonic project, it has tremendous power to impose it on the state. As the first three chapters demonstrate, big business unity on broad goals gave business the additional clout to push through the neo-liberal agenda. The trade agreements were the attempt to consolidate the transformation intended by the neo-liberal offensive and, in the words of Ambassador Jaime Zabludovsky, to make "economic reforms permanent and, thus, extended the planning horizons for domestic and foreign investors" (Grayson 2007: xi).

The Binational Evolution of NAFTA

The 1982 bank nationalization had not only spurred the Mexican bourgeoisie into great unity and assertiveness but also galvanized a relatively casual organization of Mexican and U.S. big business into a leading force for transforming Mexico and integrating Mexico's economy into that of the United States. This binational organization, the Mexico–U.S. Business Committee (MEXUS), deliberately kept a low public profile, as did the peak capitalist organizations within each of the three NAFTA countries. But along with its peak national counterparts — the CMHN (Mexico), the BCNI/CCCE (Canada) and the BRT (United States) — MEXUS played a major role in pushing NAFTA and its investment guarantees through each of the national governments.

MEXUS had been formed in 1948. It was made up of two national organizations, the Consejo Empresarial Mexicano para Asuntos Internacionales (CEMAI, Mexican Business Council for International Affairs) and the U.S.

Council, which was sponsored by the Council of the Americas, the American Chamber of Commerce of Mexico (ACCM) and the U.S. Chamber of Commerce. Each national component picked one of the co-chairpersons of MEXUS, and the organization served for three decades as an informal gathering of top U.S. and Mexican capitalists, though it had no staff and no budget until 1982. The purpose of MEXUS was to facilitate the development of a consensus on specific policies among big business in both countries, policies that would then be promoted to their respective governments by each business association.

George Grayson's *The Mexico–U.S. Business Committee* is filled with great admiration for the committee and the important role it played in the creation of NAFTA. Grayson draws on interviews with MEXUS participants as well as primary documents that MEXUS made available to him. Grayson argues that the importance of MEXUS (and we would add the CMHN, the BCNI/CCCE and the BRT) has been overlooked due to their policy of deliberately keeping a low profile. Big business did not want to be seen as meddling in state affairs: "MEXUS' informal credo was 'Let's Try to Avoid Publicity,' recalled one Mexican stalwart, who noted that the group circulated its ideas via 'non-papers' — memoranda without cover sheets or letterhead" (Grayson 2007: 8–9).

Big business has had tremendous success in reshaping society while keeping a low profile. They have been helped by newspapers and radio and TV stations, themselves owned by big business, who rarely report on the powerful role of peak business organizations in shaping government policy. In the world of the corporate media, there are "labour bosses" but no capitalist bosses. And universities, foundations and think tanks, while varying in their degree of political and intellectual pluralism, are themselves largely controlled by big business and their governmental allies. Thus we have massive schools of management and small, if any, departments of labour studies in universities today.

The state does have varying degrees of autonomy at different moments, depending on the correlation of class forces as well as the degree of conflict and consensus within the capitalist class. But the state does not act independently of the power of capital. The many accounts of the neo-liberal offensive and the development of NAFTA that focus exclusively on governmental policy, albeit with some influence from business lobby groups, obscure the central role played by the structural and instrumental power of capital in bringing about those policies.

We share Grayson's view of the central role of big business in the reshaping of North America, though not his positive appraisal of the consequences:

> Politicians and other public servants lagged far behind many corporate executives, bankers, and lawyers in advancing the concept of

a continental free-trade zone that stretches from the Yukon to the Guatemalan border and now encompasses 435 million people whose combined gross domestic income exceeds $13 trillion. Indeed, without the continual lobbying of the Mexico–U.S. Business Committee in the 1980s, the negotiation of NAFTA in the 1990s would have been unlikely, if not impossible. The bilateral committee acted like a polar force to affect the tides of economic integration. (Grayson 2007: 9)

The turn towards NAFTA had been preceded by a long period of quiet, reciprocal exchanging of ideas and strategizing between key officials of the Mexican government and U.S. business. Robert Rubin, at that time of Goldman Sachs, had been an advisor on hedge funds to Carlos Salinas in the 1980s, when Salinas was Mexico's secretary of planning and the budget. The relationship was kept secret so that Salinas would not seem to be under Wall Street's influence, and Rubin's connection with Salinas would continue after Salinas became president of Mexico in 1988. Also, in late 1984, two future Mexican presidents (Salinas and Zedillo) and one future top cabinet member (Pedro Aspe) made several trips to New York City to work with U.S. members of MEXUS on developing closer economic ties. These trips played an important role in the process leading to NAFTA. As Guy Erb, Executive Director of the U.S. Council of MEXUS, said, "[They] helped us jump start the work before the 1985 meeting with President de la Madrid" (quoted in Grayson 2007: 84–85).

According to Frederick Mayer, former aide to Senator Bill Bradley, an ardent promoter of NAFTA, Salinas had a hand in the discussions in December 1989 that led to the BRT setting up its task force to advance trade with Mexico:

> He [Salinas] found great enthusiasm for further trade and invest-ment liberalization. At his urging, Jim Robinson, Chief Executive Officer (CEO) of American Express and Colby Chandler, CEO of Eastman Kodak, both of whose companies had experience operat-ing in Mexico, formed a task force of the Business Roundtable ... to consider ways to strengthen U.S.–Mexican trade relations and to make recommendations to both governments. (Mayer 1998: 38–39)

Mexico's Shift and NAFTA

While minds had been opened to some kind of continental economic agreement, there was still considerable reticence. The Mexican government initially responded negatively towards proposals for a free trade agreement or common market with the United States as it sought a more multilateral opening. The decision to join the General Agreement of Tariffs and Trade

(GATT) in 1986 — after choosing not to join in 1979 — did not bring forth the hoped-for economic results, and Mexico's exploration of more involvement with the European Union also had disappointing results. These disappointing forays into multilateralism contributed to President Salinas's reversal of his previous stance towards North American integration in 1989. He then opened the door to the alliance of the most powerful sectors of capital with the state to try to win over Mexican business and the Mexican population to the idea of North American free trade.

Mexico's long history of a one-party regime with great autonomous power has contributed to the tendency for NAFTA to be seen as simply a state initiative that had to be sold to a strongly protectionist business class. This view ignores the transformation, discussed in Chapter 3, that both the capitalist class and state-business relations had already gone through. This outdated view of state-business relations in Mexico has contributed to a state-centred view of Mexico's turn towards free trade. Mexico's promotion and negotiation of NAFTA was carried out by a formally integrated and co-ordinated team of the business-state bloc, which was jointly led by the leading business organizations and the top state elite (Puga 2004). This process represented more than just a combined effort; it was also a key factor in the increasing fusion of decision making by Mexico's most important business leaders and top state elites. The NAFTA process involved an elaborate integration of business leaders, state leaders and state functionaries. The massive privatizations and deregulations had already advanced the consolidation of a bloc composed of state elites and top capitalists. Unlike the "transitional period" (Puga 2004: 64) described in Chapter 3, the NAFTA process was not tripartite but bipartite and binational. The *charro* labour leadership was lined up to support NAFTA but was marginalized from the negotiations and decision-making by a regime that increasingly involved direct bourgeois domination.

Carlos Salinas had been elected president in a transparently fraudulent election in 1988. Nevertheless, he still had the semi-dictatorial powers of old-regime Mexican presidents, but he faced a crisis of legitimacy because of the electoral fraud. His main — and unexpected — electoral opposition came from a nationalist candidate that had split from the ruling party and was backed by most of the Mexican Left. This opposition not only challenged the legitimacy of the presidential election but also strongly opposed continental integration. The Mexican government and the peak business organizations within Mexico conducted a campaign in favour of NAFTA that both sought to weaken opposition to NAFTA and to strengthen support for a government that had entered office with little legitimacy. The pro-NAFTA campaign argued that NAFTA was the road to prosperity and Mexico's path to becoming a First-World nation. The CMHN carried out a major campaign through newspapers, magazines, radio and television to win over small- and middle-sized businesses and the public. In 1992 alone, the CMHN spent the equivalent of $US 6.7 million on pro-NAFTA television spots throughout the whole country (Puga 2004: 129–30).

Selling NAFTA in the United States

The process of negotiating NAFTA had begun while George H.W. Bush was still president of the United States. When Bush lost the presidential election to Clinton, the Democrats retained their majorities in both the Senate and the House of Representatives. Clinton and the Democratic Congress had been elected with support from unions that strongly opposed NAFTA, and NAFTA still required the approval of the three national legislative bodies. The Clinton Administration itself was initially divided over NAFTA, but the pro-NAFTA wing defeated both those who opposed NAFTA and those who wanted to give priority to health care reform. As Hillary Clinton, an advocate of health care reform, writes in her memoirs:

> By late August [Treasury Secretary Lloyd] Bentsen, Secretary of State Warren Christopher and economic advisor Bob Rubin were adamant about postponing health care reform and moving forward with NAFTA. They believed the free trade agreement was also critical to the nation's economic recovery and NAFTA warranted immediate action. (quoted in Faux 2006: 21)

There had been very little opposition within the United States to the 1989 free trade agreement with Canada. Canada, after all, had a comparable wage structure as well as similar health, safety and environmental standards and an even stronger labour movement than that in the United States. Also, Canadians were not viewed as racially problematic. However, the proposal of a trade agreement with Mexico was another story. Mexico's low wage structure, lack of health and safety protection for workers, state-dominated unions and lax environmental standards were perceived by labour and its allies in the Democratic Party as a severe threat to U.S. jobs. And there was much opposition to NAFTA from the Right, fearing loss of sovereignty and increased migration from a non-white population, against whom there was strong and institutionalized racism in the U.S. Southwest. While accusing the anti-NAFTA forces of xenophobia, NAFTA proponents sought to assuage those fears by arguing that the trade agreement would *decrease* immigration from Mexico as more jobs would be created there (Faux 2006: 37). As well, they argued that NAFTA would bring more and better jobs to the United States. NAFTA, they argued, was not a zero-sum game, as all the economies involved would grow. And because of the purported better job skills in the United States, the better jobs would be in the United States.

When the passage of NAFTA appeared to be in trouble in the U.S. Congress, these trans-border joint efforts by government and big business culminated in the formation of the BRT's front group, the USA*NAFTA, at a meeting attended by top U.S. business people, the head of an important Mexican business lobby group and the President of Mexico himself. The meeting was called by James Robinson, the former Chair of the BRT task force on trade, and Kay Whitmore, the chair of the BRT at that time. Robinson and Whitmore brought together a set of powerful people from Mexico and the U.S. that included the President of Mexico as well as Rodman Rockefeller (head of MEXUS), Jim Jones (at that time Chair of the New York Stock Exchange, who would become U.S. Ambassador to Mexico from 1993 to 1997 and then head of MEXUS from 1997 to the present), Juan Gallardo, head of Coordinadora de Organismos Empresarios de Comercio Exterior or COECE, the Coordinating Council of Foreign Trade Business Organizations (Gallardo was also the Mexican Co-Chair of MEXUS from 1990–93), and Jerry Jaznowski (President of the National Association of Manufacturers in the U.S.). This group created USA*NAFTA "to coordinate U.S. business efforts" (Mayer 1998: 234).

The evolution and promotion of NAFTA had developed from its sponsorship by powerful government figures and business interests on both sides of the U.S.–Mexican border, with Canada joining it a bit later. But the strength of popular and congressional opposition to NAFTA in the United States galvanized business and government into a tighter and more militant joint effort to sell NAFTA. Once President Clinton made his decision to push NAFTA, the BRT and the White House began to co-ordinate their actions. This co-ordinated offensive of the Business Roundtable and the Clinton White House started with a meeting on September 14, 1993, at the Washington, D.C. headquarters of the Allied Signal corporation (MacArthur 2000). Over thirty of the top lobbyists in the United States had been called together by the tactical leadership of USA*NAFTA to participate in a campaign to sell NAFTA to Congress. One of the main organizers of the meeting, Ken Cole, chief lobbyist for Allied Signal, considered getting all these high powered, highly competitive people in one room a major accomplishment. Cole told MacArthur: "They're eagles … and you know eagles never do flock … they don't like to come together. We selected them [and] we got them" (MacArthur 2000: 168–69). Their reticence to flock together was overcome by the influence of their clients, members of the BRT.

The purpose of the meeting was to enlist the lobbyists to work on congressmen and senators that were wavering, hesitant or opposed to NAFTA. President Clinton was represented by his NAFTA team of Mickey Kantor (Clinton's campaign chair and later his trade representative), White House aide Rahm Emanuel and William Daley, who had recently been appointed as special counsel to co-ordinate an action campaign to get NAFTA passed by Congress. Nick Calio, a lobbyist himself, represented USA*NAFTA at the meeting. Calio had been congressional liaison for President George H.W. Bush. He later formed a lobbying company with "Lawrence O'Brien, III, son of the late Lawrence O'Brien, Jr., famously Democratic National Committee Chairman at the time of Watergate and confidant of John F. Kennedy" (MacArthur 2000: 169). Calio described the meeting to MacArthur:

> We basically went to [Business Roundtable] companies and told them, "Get your folks to show up." We had some trouble, as I recall, [and so we] got to the companies and said, "Tell your consultants to either show up, or they're screwed." We had literally millions of dollars worth of lobbying talent in a single room. They were, as Cole put it, "the best of the best ... the ones that have the biggest retainers from the biggest companies." (MacArthur 2000: 169)

This group of lobbyists certainly had clout, as MacArthur points out:

> The point, said Calio, was to bring "together a group of us who had been in the political process for a long time and had various jobs who knew people very, very well on a personal level, and who could talk on that level, *and by happenstance, people who had probably raised an awful lot of money for a lot of members and were part of their political life-support system, so to speak.*" (MacArthur 2000: 172, emphasis added by MacArthur)

And Rahm Emanuel, now Mayor of Chicago and former chief of staff to President Obama, made clear that reticence to carry out the campaign would not go unnoticed:

> The message to the lobbying elite, said Emanuel, was "Look, your bosses are for this, so stop fucking bad-mouthing us. It's not helping." As the campaign progressed over the next two months, "we would rat on somebody if they started screwing up." (MacArthur 2000: 172)

The Mexican government played a very direct role in the battle within the United States over NAFTA. Democratic, Republican and bipartisan lobbying firms were hired by Mexico to win over congressmen and to try to cool out popular fears. Mexican government sources state that Mexico spent $US26 million on lobbying for NAFTA between 1990 and 1993 while Mayer puts the figure "well over $30 million U.S." (Puga 2004: 194–5; Mayer 1998: 236). The combined efforts of the Mexican and U.S. governments, along with those of the Business Roundtable through USA*NAFTA, may have made the pro-NAFTA campaign the most advertised policy issue ever (MacArthur 2000: 222).

Again, one year after NAFTA, the Business Roundtable, in alliance with Clinton, pushed through joining the World Trade Organization (WTO) with the same purposes as NAFTA, but with a global scope:

> Democrat Anne Wexler ran the "grassroots" campaign of the Business Roundtable, organizing 220 CEOs to lobby lawmakers from states and districts in which their business facilities were located. Boeing spoke for the aerospace industry and Washington state, Monsanto for chemicals and Missouri, and Warner-Lambert for pharmaceuticals and New Jersey. As with NAFTA, the Democratic administration did the heavy lifting. "You have to imagine the Alice in Wonderland quality of this," a frustrated administration official told the *New York Times*. "Here we are, trying to figure out how to get business leaders to put pressure on Republicans to vote for something Reagan championed and Bush almost implemented." (Faux 2006: 159)

Business Gets Directly Involved: Trade Advisory Groups

As well as promoting NAFTA, big business shaped its content. Each country had trade advisory groups (TAG) drawn from the business sector. In the U.S. and Canadian cases, they were appointed by their governments. In the Mexican case, the Mexican business sector appointed its own committee, the COECE (Coordinadora de Organismos Empresarios de Comercio Exterior, the Coordinating Council of Foreign Trade Business Organizations). The Advisory Committee on Trade Policy and Negotiations (ACTPN) for the United States was headed by the co-chairs of the Business Roundtable's task force on trade, Jim Robinson and Kay Whitmore (Mayer 1998: 114). While actual negotiations had to be conducted between government officials, the business advisory groups would often be in another room in the same hotel, close at hand to be consulted and to give their advice. Of course, they were not mere advisors (Puga 2004: 158–62). Jeffrey Garten, Clinton's undersecretary of commerce, underscores the power of the advisors: "The executive branch depends almost entirely on business for technical information regarding trade negotiations." Furthermore, Garten "observed that American firms had become 'de facto agents of foreign policy'" (Faux 2006: 15–16). As Faux goes on to point out, all three governments took the line that it was appropriate to have business advise the government on business-related issues and exclude the rest of society:

None of the three governments permitted their trade unions, environmental groups, or other civil society organizations to become seriously involved in the negotiating process. All three had a common line: trade agreements were business matters, and each nation's interests would be taken care of by business lawyers and consultants who were to approve, reject, or amend the proposed language during the day — and in the evening bond with the negotiators over drinks and dinner. (Faux 2006: 16)

Bills of Rights for Capital

The offensive of big business against the working class in all three NAFTA countries had domestic, continental and international dimensions. The "free trade" agreements of 1989 and 1994 were aimed primarily at disciplining governments, present and future, from having policies that jeopardized the interests of capital. This was a special concern in regard to Mexico, where the combination of extreme poverty, inequality and repression have historically combined with populist and revolutionary historical traditions to pose a potential threat to the sacred rights of capital. CUFTA and NAFTA are fundamentally bills of rights for capital and chains on the democratic rights of the population as they locked in the neo-liberal policies of the three regimes from future governmental change. The costs of opting out of these treaties are astronomical, but so are the costs of remaining in them. Capital normally, by its very structure and dynamics, sets limits on democratic power by proactively attempting to shape the boundaries of the "possible." Even reformist governments generally capitulate in anticipation of the likely responses of capital. But should a government have the will and the base to move forward in spite of the responses of capital, it will face a confrontation and likely short-term crisis. Politicians focused on either careers or short-term reforms will not likely want to risk a showdown with capital. This normal power of capital within national societies has been further consolidated through international treaties, through continental or international "constitutionalization" of the rights of capital.

The capitalist classes of North America have reorganized their states to serve their interests more directly and more fully. They and their political representatives have also developed international institutions and mechanisms for constraining any alternative directions for the governments of the three states. While different interests and cleavages exist among North American capitalists, they are relatively united around a hegemonic project of crushing resistance to their main objective of turning all of the Earth into profit streams.

The devastating consequences of the capitalist offensive for the working class, the environment and society in general in all three countries are beyond the scope of our analysis here. They have been well documented in many works (Dion, Marier, Rasmus, Workman, for example). They were not incidental effects of some impersonal process, but were deliberately promoted policies to turn the state into a more direct instrument of capital accumulation and to undermine, if not destroy, organizations of collective resistance. Even the recent financial crisis of capitalism is being used to sharply deepen the offensive. Those leading the attack on government spending rarely mention subsidies for corporations or the massive public spending for the military-industrial complex. Nor does the attack on public-sector workers ever compare their modest salaries and benefits to the exorbitant salaries and benefits of the rich. The deficits created by the tax cuts for the rich, the rescue packages for banks and investors and the imperial wars of Canada and the United States are being used as a rationale for cutting the living standards of the vast majority of the population by cuts to public spending and attacks on public sector rights, jobs, wages and pensions. And in the case of Mexico, there has been an unprecedented increase in spending for internal military activities for the drug war, the low intensity war against the Zapatistas in Chiapas and a general militarization of the country to try to put a lid on popular protests. The drug war is used as the justification for this massive increase in spending for national security, which is now 2.3 percent of Mexico's GDP and is unusual for a country not engaged in regional or international conflicts. In addition to these expenditures by the Mexican government, the U.S. has provided hundreds of millions of dollars to militarize Mexico through "Plan Mexico" (also known as the Mérida Initiative), an agreement signed by the two governments on October 22, 2007, also, ostensibly, to fight drugs (Fitzpatrick-Behrens 2009; Ribando Seelke 2009). At the same time, as both the Mexican and U.S. governments spend enormous amounts on the militarization of Mexico, social spending per capita in Mexico has declined since the beginning of the neo-liberal offensive in 1982. For example, spending on education in the federal budget has declined from 3.54 percent to 1.66 percent of the GDP between 1982 and 2008 (Centro de estudios de las Finanzas Públicas, Consejo de Diputados: 2012).

The working class and labour movements of the three countries have not developed an alternative transformatory project to the one being imposed on them through the corporate offensive. They continue to resist the effects of the offensive with old tactics, strategies and institutional responses that once worked for specific groups within the working class. But the corporate offensive continues to change the whole cultural and institutional complex. The new forms of financialization and production alongside the new international treaties doom sector-by-sector defensive struggles to failure. New ways of organizing, new types of organizations and new strategies are necessary as part of a transformatory project that will challenge capitalist power in all three states.

Trans-border working-class relations in North America are not a new phenomenon. There have, in fact, been two very different and long-standing sets of working-class binational relations in North America. Mexican and U.S. workers (which include many people of Mexican ancestry) have been integrated at the labour market level as well as through cross-border production. Successive generations of Mexican workers have been integrated into the U.S. working class as well, generally in subordinate sectors. They joined the descendants of those Mexicans already present when the United States seized half of Mexico in the Mexican-American War of 1848–50. As well as those Mexican workers residing in the United States, millions of Mexicans work in plants just across the border, plants that are an integrated part of a continental production system. But there are no cross-border unions between Mexico and the United States. On the other hand, Canadian and U.S. workers have been integrated through common international unions since the nineteenth century. And while Canadian labour migration to the United States has been very small in the last half century, private sector Canadian and U.S. workers have been — and many continue to be — members of common "international" ("continental") unions.

PART II

THE TWO BINATIONALISMS

Immigrants, Workers and Unions

Chapter 5

Mexican Immigration and the U.S. Labour Market

The Continental Corporate Offensive and Immigration

Migration from countryside to city, from one country to another, was a fundamental mechanism of social mobility for most of the twentieth century. It allowed people to escape from severe poverty and oppression. But it has now become a simple conveyor belt between sweatshops of the different regions of the globe, particularly in the NAFTA region. The modern "pariahs" arrive with the chains of illegality on them. Their flight brings them back to the point of departure, but in a more legally precarious situation and in a new cultural context. The curse of poverty follows them to their "new" life. This is the social condition of present-day globalization. For poor workers and peasants, globalization is a global condemnation. It is not the movement of poor people to new countries that is the cause of growing poverty in their new homes. On the contrary, the growing poverty in the countries of origin and in the countries of destination demonstrate the emergence of a particular form of capitalist exploitation that has reconfigured the world labour market. This restructured global labour market undermines the old social basis for collective cohesion and resistance to attacks by capital. This new situation facilitates the downward harmonization of wages and working conditions globally.

For migrants, neo-liberal globalization involves exchanging one kind of suffering for another. On one side of the U.S.–Mexican border, migrants had suffered the poverty of near-starvation and the absence of basic services for themselves and their families. On the other side of the border, their poverty rises towards U.S. poverty levels, but they endure the pitiless appropriation of their life energies and bodies in the machinery of U.S. production in order to keep themselves and their families from sinking below the poverty line. In the course of this exchange of suffering, they also endure alienation from their roots as well as the racism of their host country.

The corporate offensive in Mexico is driving Mexicans to the United States to take up jobs that have already been downgraded and de-unionized by the U.S. corporate offensive. The corrosion of the labour market has continued in both "good" times and "bad." In "good" times, big business and its governmental allies argue that downward harmonization is necessary for corporations to remain globally competitive. In "bad" times, they add the argument that they just can't afford to pay decent wages to survive. In both the "good" and "bad" times, workers pay through declining wages, conditions and collective rights.

This is a far cry from the earlier situation where "good" times provided the basis for labour to make collective gains. The union movement prepared the ground for its own defeat and that of the working class by an almost exclusive focus on the economic interests of its own members and the neglect, if not abandonment, of fighting for class-wide interests. This model of unionism did not grasp the ideological and political character of the class war unleashed on the working class by neo-liberalism. Most unions continued to respond in narrow, sectoral ways that did not promote class-wide solidarity and consciousness. These policies isolated unionized workers from the non-unionized poor and precariously employed whose interests seemed marginal to unions. This narrow approach to workers' struggles unintentionally facilitated the divide-and-rule attacks of the corporate offensive. It left both the organized and unorganized sectors of the working class vulnerable to isolation from each other, as the corporate offensive picked them off segment by segment, private versus public, "respectable" workers versus the stigmatized poor, citizen versus non-citizen. The narrow, economistic and sectional focus of most unions contributed to the demise of solidarity and class consciousness.

The more marginal and precarious sections of the work force play an important role for capital in responding to the rhythms of capitalist labour demand as well as facilitating competition and conflict in the working class. Capital needs a certain amount of unemployment. A surplus of workers gives businesses flexibility and leverage to exert a downward pressure on wages and benefits. Firms, sectors and the economy as a whole have an uneven rhythm of production. Workers are needed at times and not needed at other times as the cycle rises and falls. Individual firms want workers when they need them but do not want to pay wages and benefits to the workers when they do not. A reserve supply of labour helps capitalism solve this dilemma. They can be hired and paid when needed and discarded when not needed. The costs of their survival, until needed again, are externalized, passed on to the state, where there is a social safety net, such as welfare or unemployment insurance, or to family and friends. Aside from the need to have workers when they are needed to avoid missing profit opportunities, capital wants cheap, productive and disciplined workers. As well as creating an upward pressure on wages, labour shortages contribute to a feeling of independence and possible insubordination on the part of workers. Thus, from the point of view of capital, a reserve army of labour is important not only for having labour when it is needed but also for having the kind of labour that is wanted. While there are a variety of sources for the reserve army of labour, the desperate plight of Mexicans and their lack of citizenship rights have made them a very attractive pool of disposable workers.

The use of cheap, vulnerable labour to cut wages, intensify exploitation and promote concessions is not a new phenomenon. This practice did not arrive with neo-liberal globalization but, in fact, it has a long history at local, regional and national levels. Modern technology has made this strategy more feasible and the tremendous disparities between the rich and the poor countries have made it very attractive. Recurrent economic problems since the 1970s as well as the strength of labour in the 1960s in the rich countries intensified its appeal even further.

Thus, immigration is not the cause of the decline in workers' rights and livelihoods in the United States and Canada any more than is the mass entry of other groups of the reserve army of labour into the labour force. The utilization of poorer, more marginal or racially stigmatized workers to undermine the power of other workers is an old tool of capital. The use of different segments of the domestic or the external reserve army of labour is a matter of circumstances and convenience for capital. The informal globalization of the labour force has created an increasingly global reserve army of labour that capitalism seeks to use as one of its many tools to intensify competition between workers, decrease the wages and rights of workers and increase discipline over workers. Unauthorized immigrants — as compared to citizen members of the reserve army of labour — have a special attraction to capital in that they have little recourse to legal challenges to exploitation and, with the aid of state agencies, can be more easily intimidated. As well, they can be disposed of when no longer needed. While all workers are disposable, non-authorized foreign workers can be deported as well as fired. Deportation has been used on a massive scale when immigrant workers have no longer been needed. The cost of maintaining unemployed workers and their families can be passed back to the sending country, which has already paid the costs of (re)producing this sector of the labour force, and nativist racism can be utilized to deflect popular discontent from capital to immigrant workers. Both the massive recruitment and massive deportation of Mexicans has been a recurrent phenomenon in U.S. history.

Migration, both internal and international, and plant relocation have been two of the most important methods of incorporating cheap, vulnerable labour into the modern capitalist production process. The migration of poor African Americans and poor whites from the southern U.S. to the north in the first half of the twentieth century, the migration of Mexicans from the poorer states to the industrial zones around Mexico City in earlier periods and to the northern *maquila* zones in recent times and the migration of Canadians from the poorer eastern provinces to industrial centres in the past and to the Alberta oil zones more recently are examples of internal migration. Plant relocation has taken place from the U.S. northeast and midwest — now called the Rust Belt — to the anti-union, "right-to-work" states of the south and southwest and from the old industrial zones around Mexico City to the northern *maquilas* zones of Mexico.

International migration, long a source of labour, has been intensified by the devastating impact of neo-liberal policies on poorer countries. Masses of desperate, impoverished people seek to reach the promised lands of the "rich" countries to sell their labour power so that they and their families and home communities can survive. Many of these unauthorized migrants suffer great brutalization, humiliation and hardship on their journeys to new countries, journeys that they are often not able to complete. Advances in technology have made possible the further extension of factory locations to the home countries of cheap, vulnerable labour, though with great costs of environmental destruction related to the transportation of materials and goods. Plant relocation has brought its own horrors of super-exploitation, environmental pollution and increases in work-related health hazards, often hidden in antiseptic, modern-looking facilities. The corporate offensive of the last forty years has changed the face of the globe, forced millions to move from one form of poverty to another, destroyed families and communities and spread toxic waste and environmental destruction. The poor and working people of the rich and the poor countries are paying a huge price for the relentless pursuit of profit and competitive advantage while the rich and super-rich get even richer as the world edges towards the environmental abyss.

The corporate offensive in all three North American countries had devastating effects on the lives of ordinary working people. Unions were severely weakened, collective bargaining undermined, real wages pushed down and the social net sharply weakened. NAFTA sought to consolidate, deepen and extend the gains of the most powerful sections of the capitalist class of each country through treaties that were intended to be almost impossible to change. Continental integration was a continuation of the class war of key sectors of capital against their own societies and working classes.

The threat and practice of factory relocation to Mexico plays a similar role to that of the decades of factory relocation to the American south and southwest. It serves as a downward pressure on workers' rights, working conditions and wages in the wealthier and more unionized regions or countries. The greater disparity between Mexico on the one hand and the United States and Canada on the other makes the threat to workers and the benefits to capital even greater. As well, Mexico is the source of massive numbers of unauthorized and thereby vulnerable workers. The Mexican labour force has long served as a reserve army of labour for U.S. capitalism

— workers that are recruited when needed and expelled when no longer needed. But migration has now become more permanent — and less cyclical and temporary — given the strength of the push of workers out of Mexico, the increased border security that heightens the risk of border crossing, the present depth of the cross-border networks between the United States and Mexico and the enormous size of the authorized and non-authorized immigrant communities.

An understanding of the radical demographic change in the western hemisphere is necessary in order to grasp the basis for the enormity of this wave of human migration. Economic crisis and restructuring provide the push for the massive emigration towards the United States. But the magnitude of this migration is based on the demographic transformation of the western hemisphere. There has been an inversion of the population ratio between the United States and Latin America from the beginning of the last century to the beginning of this century. Early in the twentieth century, there were more people living in the United States than in all of Latin America. In 1914, the United States had a population of one hundred million, while all of Latin America had only eighty million, and most lived in rural areas (Maddison 2001: 183, 193). Ninety-six years later, the numbers were dramatically reversed. In 2010, Latin America had a population almost double that of the United States, with 590 million people living in Latin America (CEPAL/ECLAC 2011: 212) as compared to approximately 308.8 million in the United States (U.S. Census Bureau 2011f).

The tremendous demographic expansion has meant that great numbers of new jobs had to be created in Mexico to absorb the new entrants to the labour force. Instead, the corporate offensive has destroyed great numbers of relatively good jobs, produced more precarious and even lower paid work and dismantled the very limited social net as well as numerous sources of survival in the rural sector. Rural subsistence agriculture as well as most stable, relatively well-paid jobs — a small minority of all jobs in the first place — have been destroyed, replaced only by precarious work with wages insufficient to support a family, even with several family members working. Mexicans are migrating in vast numbers for their very survival and that of their families. Remittances — money sent from workers in the U.S. to family members back home — are the sole source of subsistence for many communities in Mexico. Emigration from Mexico did not start with the recent corporate offensive. But the offensive in Mexico so intensified and extended poverty that the desperation level and size of the migration grew sharply. The downward spiral of working-class conditions, wages and collective organization in all three countries is the result of the capitalist offensive that precedes the recent massive migration of Mexicans to the United States. Whether or not — and to what extent — this massive migration contributes to a continuation of this downward spiral in the United States can only be judged within the context of the character of the class struggle at various moments, the relative balance of class forces, the strategies of corporations and those of unions and the workers movement more generally. The impact of migration on workers' rights, conditions and organization is historically contingent.

The promise of some employment, albeit at the bottom of the corroded occupational ladder, in the United States has continued to attract Mexican workers. This attraction has intensified as the wage differential between Mexico and the United States has grown with each peso devaluation and with the ongoing fall of real wages in Mexico. A self-sustaining labour recruitment infrastructure has developed based on generations of previous migrants and the physical contiguity of Mexico and the United States. This self-sustaining system meshes with and is made possible by the embedded nature of this source of labour for sectors of U.S. industry (Cornelius 1998).

The use of the threat or practice of relocation as a tool of capital to cut costs and to discipline workers is not new nor is it unique to cross-border or international situations (Cowie 1999; Bronfenbrenner 1997). It did not suddenly appear with NAFTA. Plant relocation has long been a weapon in capital's struggle against workers. Jefferson Cowie (1999) has described this well in his study of RCA, in which he traces RCA's moves from Camden, New Jersey, to Bloomington, Indiana, to Memphis, Tennessee, and finally to Ciudad Juárez to escape unions and keep wages down. The wage disparities between the different regions in the United States pale in comparison to those between Mexico and its two northern neighbours. These disparities, as well as the fiercely — and sometimes violent — repression that union organizing faces both in Mexico and the southern U.S., motivated RCA's moves.

The threat and practice of relocation as a weapon against workers has been made all the more effective by its extension into labour markets with greater poverty, more surplus labour and a more repressive state. The spectre of poor Mexicans "stealing" the jobs of United States and Canadian workers has now been joined by the spectre of poor Chinese "stealing" the jobs of North American workers, including Mexicans. The race to the bottom in terms of wages, working conditions and democratic rights of workers is relentless. But it is not a race propelled by the "natural" workings of the market. It is being shaped and propelled by corporate and governmental policies that express themselves in actions ranging from plant-level threats and intimidation to international treaties and new international organizations that can even discipline governments.

Relocation has always been an effective tool as both a threat and a practice through which capital could control, defeat or discard troublesome labour. Traditional union methods are ineffective against relocation, especially when governments join with companies in blocking worker organization in the new locations. The greater instability of employment (location, duration, security) is also a strong obstacle to the efficacy of traditional forms of union organization as a tool of collective resistance. The casualization of labour fragments the working class and obscures their common situation. Sub-contracting, hiring workers through temporary employment agencies, creating several categories of workers (casual and permanent) and other devices all undermine the basis of collective resistance that previously existed in workplaces with a relatively stable labour force.

Plant relocation as well as migration involves the incorporation of pauperized Mexican labour into the North American labour market. The tool of plant relocation is wielded by capital against labour *within* Mexico as well as *within* the United States and Canada. Further, the threat and practice of moving to even cheaper and more vulnerable reserve armies of labour in southern Mexico, Central America and China shows the self-defeating character of competing for jobs by offering cheap, flexible and non-union labour or by entering into productivity alliances with companies.

Vulnerable migration and plant relocation are both tools of capitalists in their never-ending offensive against workers. These practices have been part of the move to the neo-liberal regulation of labour, which includes increased management power over workers (often misnamed as "labour flexibility"), lean production, weakened or destroyed unions, lower wages and deteriorated health and safety standards and practices. This assault on workers' rights, wages and working and living conditions did not start with NAFTA, but NAFTA deepened, widened and gave international treaty support to these neo-liberal practices. Neo-liberalism and NAFTA are aimed at reducing labour costs and increasing labour discipline and productivity.

The labour market and labour movements of North America continue to be transformed by neo-liberal reforms and free trade agreements that facilitate the restriction of labour rights, by the intensification of migration from Latin America that has resulted from these reforms and by the continental relocation and geographic reorganization of production. Precarious migration by Mexicans to North America and the shifting of production to Mexico contribute to the downward pressure on the labour market and on working conditions in the United States and Canada. Emigration from Mexico has not been slowed down by these plant relocations as they are part of a package of neo-liberal reforms that destroy more jobs and sources of livelihood in Mexico than they create.

The Continental Corporate Offensive, the Race to the Bottom and Immigration

Brecht, Greenspan and a Little History,
or The Dirty Little Secret of High Tech Growth

Who built Thebes of the seven gates?
In the books you will read the names of kings.
Did the kings haul up the lumps of rock?

And Babylon, many times demolished,
Who raised it up so many times?

In what houses of gold glittering Lima did its builders live?
Where, the evening that the Great Wall of China was finished, did
    the masons go?

Great Rome is full of triumphal arches.
Who erected them?

Over whom did the Caesars triumph?
Had Byzantium, much praised in song, only palaces for its inhabitants?

Even in fabled Atlantis, the night that the ocean engulfed it,
The drowning still cried out for their slaves.

The young Alexander conquered India.
Was he alone?

Caesar defeated the Gauls.
Did he not even have a cook with him?

Philip of Spain wept when his armada went down.
Was he the only one to weep?

Frederick the 2nd won the 7 Years War.
Who else won it?

Every page a victory.
Who cooked the feast for the victors ?

Every 10 years a great man.
Who paid the bill?

So many reports.

So many questions.
(Brecht 1935)

In his speech to the National Governors Association (NGA), "Structural Change in the New Economy," the legendary President of the Federal Reserve Board of the United States, Alan Greenspan (2000), celebrated the most prolonged economic expansion in the history of the United States (1992–2000) which, in his view, flowed from the irresistible power of competition and the growth of the efficiency of corporations: "States with more flexible labour markets, skilled work forces, and a reputation for supporting innovation and entrepreneurship will be prime locations for firms at the cutting edge of technology" (Greenspan: 2000). Alan Greenspan's comparison of the United States and Europe hailed the unilateral control of labour market flexibility by corporations as the key to U.S. economic superiority. In elaborating the reasons for U.S. prosperity, he concluded:

> An intriguing aspect of the recent wave of productivity acceleration is that U.S. businesses and workers appear to have benefited more from the recent advances in information technology than their counterparts in Europe or Japan. Those countries ... have also participated ... but they appear to have been slower to exploit it. The relatively inflexible and, hence, more costly labour markets of these economies appear to be a significant part of the explanation. The elevated rates of return offered by the newer technologies in the United States are largely the result of a reduction in labour costs per unit of output. The rates of return on investment in the same new technologies are correspondingly less in Europe and Japan because businesses there face higher costs of displacing workers than we do. Here, labour displacement is more readily countenanced both by law and by culture. Parenthetically, because our costs of dismissing workers are lower, the potential costs of hiring and the risks associated with expanding employment is less. The result of this significantly higher capacity for job dismissal has been, counter intuitively, a dramatic decline in the U.S. unemployment rate in recent years. (Greenspan 2000)

In the months after the signing of NAFTA, Greenspan was obsessed with its possible effects on prices and labour costs (Woodward 2011: 246). However, productivity increased at the same time that unemployment surprisingly decreased without provoking a shift in the balance of power in the U.S. labour market in favour of workers. The concern about a potentially tight labor market and its effect on the wages and the balance of power between clases was not insignificant, given that labour costs represented 70 percent of the operating costs of the U.S. economy. The explanation of this surprising outcome is found in the greater insecurity of workers and the greater flexibility of management in hiring and firing, which Greenspan so highly praised.

Furthermore, labour insecurity was rooted in an unusual scissor effect: the simultaneous presence of an accelerated rate of technological change and the incorporation of a pool of new workers in conditions of extreme vulnerability (the millions of Mexican workers who entered the U.S. labour market in those years) into the labour force. One important result of the Mexican crisis of 1994 was that the tendencies in the Mexican and U.S. labour markets criss-crossed: whereas the reserve army of labour in the U.S. decreased continuously in the thirty-six months following 1984, with unemployment declining from 9.6 million to 6.2 million, the mass of unemployed workers in Mexico rose from 2.8 million to 4.6 million (Anuario Estadístico de los EUM 2002: 223). Mexico's method of measuring unemployment, in fact, greatly underestimates real unemployment.

The 1994 Mexican crisis produced masses of newly unemployed workers in one fell swoop. The opening of the migratory floodgates in 1995 alleviated the labour shortage for the booming U.S. economy. The incorporation of this surplus labour force into the U.S. labour market, a labour force that was without labour rights or union organization, was fundamental for the prolongation of the profitability of U.S. corporations over the next four years.

The Mexican crisis of 1994, from this perspective, was not a minor or insignificant factor in maintaining the general rate of profit of the U.S. economy. The U.S. economy had begun to experience a sharp scarcity of unemployed workers. This tight labour market had the potential of undermining labour discipline and contributing to an upward pressure on wages. The Mexican crisis alleviated this problem by expelling millions of workers who replenished the reserve army of labour in the United States and played an essential role for the growing U.S. economy at this time.

The global high-tech industry depended on the service sector for those necessary activities that allowed it to function both smoothly and profitably. The Hispanic labour force continued contributing in a decisive manner to the momentum of the U.S. economy by providing that fundamental supply of human resources needed in sectors such as services and infrastructure. Mexicans made up most of the six million additional Latina/o workers that were absorbed, in a permanent or temporary manner in the first eight years of the twenty-first century by the insatiable growth of housing, services and cities. The 40 percent increase in Hispanic workers in the United States from 2000–8 prevented the links between the two roads of the U.S. economy, that of internationalized, high-tech industry and that of domestic, intensive and low wage labour, from being overstrained and overheated by the scarcity of cheap labour. The high-tech sector rests on daily maintenance by millions of low-tech, poorly paid workers.

The crucial role of immigrant labour in the development of U.S. capitalism is not new, and Mexican workers have always been an important source. During World War I, when the United States faced labour shortages, the government adopted the Temporary Admission Program to import cheap Mexican labour for U.S. industry and agriculture. During the Great Depression of the 1930s, massive numbers of Mexicans were deported by the U.S. government. Estimates range from several hundred thousand to over a million (Kanstroom 2007: 215; Gutiérrez 1995: 72–75, Meier and Ribera 1993: 153–58). Again, with labour shortages during World War II and the Korean War, the U.S. and Mexican governments formally agreed to the Bracero Program, a program on temporary contract labour. The U.S. needed workers and the Mexican government hoped that the formalization of labour contracts would reduce the extreme exploitation of Mexican workers that entered the country informally (Meier and Ribera 1993: 173–84). And again, in the period of 1954–55, the U.S. government carried out its "Operation Wetback," in which several million Mexicans were deported. Estimates of the number deported range from one million to almost four million:

> This concern [union organizing and subversive influences] (among others) led to Operation Wetback, a government campaign that forcibly repatriated 1 to 2 million Mexicans in 1954 – some having crossed without documents, others holding bracero contracts, still others U.S. citizens or longtime residents. (Cohen 2011: 42)

The term "wetback" is a derogatory term used to label Mexicans by U.S. whites, especially in the southwest. The term refers to an image of Mexicans crossing the Rio Grande River, the border between Texas and Mexico. As late as 1951, the President's Commission on Migratory Labor in American Agriculture used this disparaging term in its final report:

> The wetback is a Mexican national who, figuratively, if not literally, wades or swims the Rio Grande. Whether he enters by wading or swimming, crawls through a hole in a fence, or just walks over a momentarily unguarded section of the long land border, he is a wetback. Since he enters by evading the immigration officers, he is, in any event, an illegally entered alien. The term wetback is widely accepted and used without derision; hence for convenience, it is used here. (quoted in Reimers 1992: 58)

The argument that this pejorative term was used without derision shows the depth of racist attitudes in these discussions.

There was a diminished flow of immigration to the U.S. for the next ten years (1955–65), but it picked up steam again in the second half of the 1960s and even more so since the 1970s. The density of community and family links between Mexicans on one side of the border and Mexican-Americans and Mexicans on the other side creates powerful networks for cross-border labour mobility. The deep crises of the Mexican economy since the 1970s as well as the devastating neo-liberal restructuring have intensified the push of workers out of Mexico while the insatiable desire of U.S. employers for cheap and vulnerable labour has created ample opportunities, and business pressure groups have been successful in creating legal loopholes in policies intended to regulate or stop undocumented immigration. The "Texas Proviso" provides a good example of the effectiveness of the agribusiness lobby. President Truman and the American Federation of Labor sought to pass legislation in the early 1950s to outlaw the employment of undocumented immigrants However, the legislation that was enacted kept the doors open for the use of cheap, expendable immigrant workers:

> Senator James Eastland of Mississippi, a staunch supporter of the national origins quotas and limited immigration and an opponent of refugee bills like the Displaced Persons Act, was tolerant about admitting undocumented aliens. He insisted the Douglas amendment [i.e., to make the employment of undocumented aliens illegal] was "unfair to the farmer or the Mexican involved." Eastland had strong support in the Senate and among agri-business, and the Senate voted down the Douglas amendment. As signed into law by the President, the measure ... did nothing about those who hired undocumented workers. Instead, the law specifically said that employment of undocumented workers did not constitute "harboring."... The exception, known as the Texas Proviso, indicated a clear victory for the growers. (Reimers 1992: 51–52)

The very programs meant, in part, to contain Mexicans in Mexico continue to stimulate further migration. The *maquila* program, for example, attracts workers from other regions of Mexico to work in the frontier. Work in the *maquilas* enhances transferable skills, intensifies awareness of the great differences in wages on both sides of the border, familiarizes people with the border region as well as brings them to the edge of the "First World" (Sassen 1996; Kopinak and Soriano 2010). The ongoing tension over immigration policy and job protection has led to a variety of measures and legislation, including the increasing militarization of the border (Andreas 1998; Dunn 1996). Nevertheless, the demographic pressure, the economic disparities and the desire of business for cheap and vulnerable labour make the immigration flow uncontainable.

The U.S.–Mexican labour market grew significantly in the post-World War II years and even more sharply in the last thirty years. The *maquila* program did not deter it but, in fact, acted in a complementary manner.

NAFTA was politically promoted in the United States, in part, as a way of stopping the undocumented immigrant flow through the creation of more jobs in Mexico. But, in fact, the *maquila* program and NAFTA help complete the integration of Mexican labour into the U.S. labour market as wage and work disparities become more clear to Mexican workers in the border zones.

While NAFTA makes all of Mexico a *maquila* zone, some production still must take place closer to consumers, and less mobile capital in the United States needs to continually lower its labour costs to compete with goods now entering more and more freely from Mexico. A great volume of Latina/o workers have moved into fundamental sectors of the U.S. labour market to do the work that cannot be readily relocated. And, as mentioned above, the role of Latina/o workers in the service sector has played an essential role in making high-tech expansion possible. Latina/o workers are very important in specific sectors, both labour intensive and high tech. The Sun Belt boom in the U.S., and its expanded low-end manufacturing and service job base, were significant factors in the demand for Mexican labour. In the past, when periods of expansion were followed by periods of contraction, segments of the reserve army of labour were pushed out of the employed labour force. In the case of non-citizen Mexicans, that has meant massive deportations. The political appeal of mass deportations has increased along with the economic crisis of the U.S. However, the crucial role of Latina/o workers in the U.S. economy, make mass deportations extremely problematic from an economic standpoint.

The importance of Mexico specifically — and Latin America more generally — as a vast pool of cheap labour has mushroomed in the last decades. Large-scale immigration to the United States remains one of the highest migration flows in the world. One-in-six workers in the United States in 2010 was Latina/o and it is projected that the proportion of Latina/os in the U.S. workforce will increase to one-in-five by 2020 (Kochlar 2012). Latina/os continue to be the most dynamically growing sector of the working class in the world's leading capitalist power. The Latina/o population has been rapidly increasing both as a result of natural growth and migration in the last decades.

Mexicans make up 63 percent of the fifty million Latina/os in the United States as of spring 2010 (United States Census Bureau 2011: 3). Mexican labour on both sides of the border has become increasingly important to U.S. capitalism. One-in-three employed Mexican nationals are employed in the United States (Velasco and Roman 1998: 49), and one-in-four industrial workers in Mexico is employed in *maquilas* or other forms of continentally integrated production, such as auto plants (INEGI 2012). Based on these figures, we can estimate that over 58 percent of employed Mexican workers are employed continentally, either working in the United

States in all activities (industrial, services and agriculture) or in plants in Mexico that are part of a continental production process. Employment of Mexican nationals in the United States is about 50 percent of employment in Mexico itself. Some eight million Mexican nationals were employed in the United States in 2008 (U.S. Census Bureau 2011a), and there were 16.5 million jobs in the formal sector within Mexico as of 2010: 14.9 million registered in the Instituto Mexicano del Seguro Social (INEGI 2011), plus the 2.5 million registered in the Instituto de Seguridad y Servicios Sociales de los Trabajadores del Estado (State Employees' Social Security and Social Services Institute) (IMSS 2010).

The U.S. population grew by 25.6 million from 2000 to 2009, from 281 million to 306.6 million. Slightly more than half of U.S. population growth in this period, 13.1 million people, was a result of Latin American immigration (U.S. Census Bureau 2011f: 9). The Pew Research Center projects that Latin Americans will comprise ninety million of the predicted 2030 U.S. population of 380 million (Passel and Cohn 2008: 27). That is, almost one-in-four people living in the United States will be of Latin American origin. The number of Mexican nationals living in the United States is estimated to have increased from 9.1 million in 2000 to 11.7 million in 2010 (Grieco et al. 2012: Table 1, p. 33). According to these figures, one out of every ten Mexican nationals was living in the United States at the end of the first decade of the twenty-first century.[1] Additionally, Latina/os constitute a significant portion of the population of nine of the ten major cities in the United States. As of 2010, almost half of the population of the Los Angeles metropolitan area were Latina/o, (i.e., 5.7 million of a total population of 12.8 million), and there were 4.4 million Latina/os in the New York metropolitan area, which has a total population of 18.8 million (U.S. Census Bureau, Statistical Abstract of the United States 2012b: 31).

The majority of the estimated 11.2 million unauthorized immigrants living in the United States in 2010 were from Mexico (58 percent, or 6.5 million), while Latin America as a whole, including Mexico, was the source of 81 percent of unauthorized immigrants. Asia provided 11 percent, and the rest were from other areas (Passell and Cohn 2011). Neither the militarized border nor the present crisis can change the intractable reality of the transnational labour market for Mexicans. While immigration measures taken by the Obama Administration have contained undocumented migration during the three years of economic recession (2007–10) in the United States, substantial numbers of Mexicans have continued to immigrate legally to the United States, with an average of nearly 165,000 migrants a year or almost a half million (494,000) over those three years. The flow of Mexicans into the United States continues to be significant even though unauthorized migration has weakened. In the period from 2010 to 2015, another million-

and-a-half Mexicans are expected to join the Mexican communities that preceded them for a total of about fifteen million Mexican nationals in the United States by 2015 (Department of Homeland Security 2011). The rate of immigration in the U.S. by Mexicans can be expected to accelerate again when and if the U.S. economy makes a recovery, even if it is a relatively job-less recovery, as long as the long-term deterioration of the Mexican labour market continues. Even in the short term of a crisis, the dependency of the Mexican economy on the United States market means that a U.S. crisis im-mediately becomes a Mexican crisis. The loss of jobs in Mexico during a U.S. crisis will continue to push Mexicans northward even if there are fewer job opportunities in the United States.

From Third World to First World: Poverty, Crisis, More Poverty

The new waves of Mexican migrants are being incorporated into an economy that is being re-organized for integrated continental production in a neo-liberal framework. This has profound implications for the incorpora-tion of immigrants into the labour force. Earlier waves of European im-migrants made economic gains through political and trade union struggle in the context of a U.S. economy that was both growing and expanding the number of jobs. These opportunities, however, are generally blocked for Latina/os and African Americans through the practices of institutional-ized racism, which ghettoized them in job sectors of lesser opportunity. However, while the job ghettoization of Latina/os and African Americans persists, the character of the post-1970s expansion of the economy is radi-cally different: it is an expansion that, unlike earlier U.S. economic expan-sions, includes declines in wages, job security and working conditions. The opportunity structure for advancement through immigration has shrunk as the labour market has been harmonized downward in the name of international competitiveness. This deterioration of the labour market is the result of deliberate corporate and government policies. The sectors in which immigrant labour is concentrated have been the most vulnerable to restructuring, downsizing and the threat and practice of job relocation. The corporate offensive has made the process of deliberately degrading the labour market a permanent feature of capitalism, continuing apace in expansionary times and in times of crisis. Only the rationale changes from that of needing to maintain competitiveness to that of needing to survive the downturn. In either case, the health, safety and living standards of working people continue to be attacked, as does the job market and the environment.

This transformed job structure is not only the entry point for the new waves of Mexican immigrants but also the location for the previous waves of immigrants and the Mexican-American population. They remain concentrated in the low end of the employment structure. Thus, the new entrants and the various layers of previous immigrants and Mexican-Americans are being compressed together at the bottom end of a job structure, which itself is being transformed in a downward direction.

Thus the recent immigrants, the "one-and-a-half generation immigrants" (those born abroad but raised in the United States), and the second-generation immigrants are finding their prospects very bleak. The combination of the persistently large immigration flow with the deteriorating job market bodes ill for the immigrants and their children.

Some of the consequences of this deterioration in the labour market have been partially overcome by having many members of the family participate in the labour force. The cultural capacity to constitute extended family units — and the sacrifice of more and more living labour for lower and lower wages — has been the only way that Latino families have been able to pay the very high cost of housing in U.S. cities. Only combining five or six salaries within extended families makes payment of these high rents possible. A single salary, what was once called a "family wage," could not pay these high rents that, in any case, only provide overcrowded single-family housing for extended families. Sixty-eight percent of the 7.3 million Latino families who rent a home live in units with two or less bedrooms and more than one person per room. The median space per person in these units is 350 square feet, less than that of families below the poverty line, where the median is 433 square feet per person (U.S. Census Bureau 2011g).

The economic crisis that started in 2008 has intensified the decades-long deterioration of life opportunities that workers and the poor had already been experiencing. The crisis pushed many working people from modest living standards into poverty and pushed the already poor into much deeper poverty. But business survived the crisis in flying colours, with profits as well as executive salaries and benefits rising once again with the help of a massive transfer of wealth to the rich through the Bush-Obama bailouts. The "too-big-to-fail" financial institutions of the rich have been bailed out by state funds whose payback has been put on the shoulders of the general population. The crisis has not led to a reversal of neo-liberal policies in spite of the anger at the financial sector in the United States. Rather, it has been used as a new rationale for carrying out the ongoing attack on workers and the interests of the community. The governmental deficits, created by the tax cuts and the massive bailouts for the rich as well as the United States' imperial wars abroad, are now used as an excuse for the cutbacks and privatizations long argued for by the capitalist class.

The nucleus of the dominant class of U.S. capitalism, that 5 percent of the population that receives almost 22 percent of the national income in the United States and is composed of five million families with an average annual income over $3 million, has survived the crisis well. While there has been a general impoverishment of most of the U.S. population, the rich have continued to do very well. Increasing inequality, a trend already strong in the last few decades of the corporate offensive, has continued to grow sharply since the start of the 2008 crisis. The crisis reduced the share of national income of the top 5 percent slightly, to 21.3 percent, because of the decrease in the profits on investment, but income distribution in the U.S. continues to be profoundly unequal. The share of money income of the poorest 40 percent of the United States population is only 11.8 percent (U.S. Census Bureau 2011: 11).

The working poor, those employed and unemployed, whose incomes hover around or below the poverty line, make up a veritable internal reserve army of labour, people who can be hired and fired according to the ups and downs of capitalist cycles. Though the image of the poor long promoted by the media has been that of welfare-dependent, racialized minorities, especially Afro-Americans, the reality was, and is, different. Most of the poor — white, Black, Latina/o and Asian — generally worked at difficult and hazardous jobs, as most of the poor continue to do today. They are poor because they are paid poverty wages often combined with precarious, irregular employment.

The face of the poor, however, has been changing with growing immigration and the continuing victimization of the Black working and poor populations. The majority of the poor had still been whites in the 1990s. But now, Hispanics and people of colour taken together make up the majority of the poor, totalling 26.6 million of the 46.2 million poor in the United States. The remaining 19.6 million poor are white (U.S. Bureau of Census 2011c: 15). In 2010, non-citizens born outside the United States had a poverty rate of 26.7 percent. African Americans had a poverty rate of 27.4 percent, young adults (ages twenty-five to thirty-four), had a poverty rate of 21.9 percent and Hispanics a poverty rate of 26.6 percent. Poverty rates were especially high among women of colour, especially young women (U.S. Census Bureau 2011b: 61).

The proportion of Latina/os, especially Mexicans and Central Americans, among the working poor has increased dramatically from 1980 to 2010. The number of Latina/os among the poor increased from 11 percent in 1980 to 28 percent in 2008, although they only made up 16 percent of the total population in that year. In spite of the economic boom of the 1990s, the number of poor Mexicans within the United States did not cease to grow — instead it increased to 3.7 million in 1990, 5.4 million in 2000, 6.2 million in 2003 and 10.1 million in 2010 (U.S. Census Bureau 2011a: 67; U.S. Census Bureau 2011b).

Recessions have a much greater effect on poverty and unemployment among Latina/os and African Americans than they do on the general population. The normally higher rates of poverty and unemployment in these groups goes up even more sharply as a result of their greater concentration in precarious sectors of the labour market and institutionalized racism. Latina/os and African Americans have been especially hard hit in the current recession as well as in the other three post-1970 recessions.

There have been four major recessions in the post-World War II period: 1) the 1973–75 recession, precipitated by the oil shock, 2) the 1981–83 economic contraction, which accelerated the worldwide corporate offensive against workers and unions, 3) the 1990–91 recession, which was towards the end of the first Bush presidency and 4) the 2007–10 recession, which started during the second term of the younger Bush's presidency.

Only 7.5 percent (277,000) of the 3.7 million Latina/o workers in the U.S. labour force in 1973 were unemployed before the start of the recession of 1973–75 (Bureau of Labor Statistics 2011: 36). Nevertheless, their low salaries kept them in the most impoverished layer of the U.S. labour force. Twenty-two percent of the Latina/o population were below the official poverty line before the start of the recession of the mid-1970s (Bureau of Census, Historical Poverty Tables).

The economic crisis of the fall of 1973 expanded unemployment and poverty to levels not seen in the previous three decades. The general rate of unemployment increased from 4.8 percent to 8.3 percent from 1973–75. Eight million people were unemployed in 1975. But the impact on Latina/os was much sharper, where unemployment increased from 7.5 percent to 13 percent in the same period, going from 277,000 to 533,000 people. The percentage of Latina/os below the poverty line increased from 21.9 percent to 26.9 percent, trapping three million Latina/os in poverty for several months, 600,000 more than before the start of the recession.

The recession of 1981–83 had a cruel impact on the Latina/o population. Latina/o unemployment more than doubled, going from 7.7 percent at the start of the crisis to 15.7 percent in the winter of 1983, while the overall unemployment rate in 1983 was 9.8 percent. Over a million Latina/os were unemployed as of February 1983 (Bureau of Labor Statistics, n.d.a.

Poverty sharply increased in the Latino barrios and communities as a result of the combined effect of significant price rises and growing unemployment. This pushed many Latino families under the poverty line. Thirty percent of Latino families were below the poverty line in 1982. The close correlation between unemployment and poverty can be seen once again here; increased unemployment led to increased poverty, albeit with a slight lag.

Even in the less severe crises, such as those of the 1990s and 2001–2, the brief increases in unemployment were reflected immediately in a growth of poverty: Latino unemployment increased from 7.7 percent to 12 percent in the 1990–92 economic contraction while poverty rates among Latina/os rose from 26.2 to 30.6 percent.

Towards the end of 2007, the U.S. economy began to show the first signs of the economic torment to come, a torment announced by diverse economic astrologers with certain anticipation, but one which quickly acquired dimensions that made even the most pessimistic predictions pale. Already, by the summer of 2008, the unemployment rate was 5.8 percent, a point more than the year before. Nine million people were already out of work.

The year 2008 was a slow walk to the brink for Latina/o workers. Unemployment among Latina/os increased from around 1.2 million in 2007 to 1.5 million in the spring of 2008 and further to 1.9 million in that summer. Between late December 2007 and early January 2009, month by month, 100,000 Latina/o workers lost their jobs and were not able to find other ones. The percentage of unemployed among Latina/os went from 5 percent in December 2006 to 13 percent in December 2009, an increase of 8 percentage points in three years. By December 2009, there were almost three million unemployed Latina/os, the greatest number in history. For the mass of Latina/o workers, as for the working class more generally, the economic recovery has not begun.

There has also been a significant increase in part-time work among Latina/os during this crisis. Part-time employment, that is, less than thirty-five hours per week, has grown among Latina/os from 2.6 million in 2006 to 4.9 million in 2011, which represents 23 percent of employed Latina/os. This is the highest percentage since the previous severe crisis of 1993, when scarcely 14 percent of employed Latina/os were part-time. This near-doubling in the percentage of part-time workers among Latina/o workers is one of the important impacts of the crisis (Bureau of Labor Statistics, n.d.b). Though open unemployment has not reached the level of 1983, the crisis has extended and deepened poverty through the downgrading of jobs to less stable and more poorly paid ones in the supposed recovery. Part-time employment is a method for downgrading jobs and contributes to increasing poverty and insecurity. The Bureau of Labour Statistics (BLS) recognized the existence of three million Latina/os as part of the working poor in 2010. Latinas/os account for almost 30 percent of the working poor (Bureau of Labor Statistics 2012: Table 2).

Latina/os made up 20 percent of unemployed workers in 2009, while Afro-Americans had an unemployment rate close to 17 percent, which for youths between the ages of sixteen and twenty-four, rises to 32 percent. (Bureau of Labor Statistics, n.d.c). The hardest hit by unemployment at this time were Black and Latina women.

The impoverishment of immigrant workers, both documented and undocumented, in the United States has increased even more sharply than in the population as a whole as a result of the massive unemployment and reduced salaries caused by the first great recession of the twenty-first century. This impoverishment has been aggravated by the increases in the costs of many basic products. Poverty doubled from 2000 to 2010 among legal Hispanic immigrants (citizens and those with legal residency) from one million to two million people (U.S. Census Bureau 2011b: 15). Poverty was present in massive numbers in both the Latino and African American populations, with 13.2 million Latina/os and 10.7 million African Americans below the poverty line in 2010. The BLS has shown that the average income of Latino workers who are employed full-time decreased, even in nominal terms, between the first quarter of 2009 and the first quarter of 2010. The situation was even worse among Latinas employed full-time, whose average income fell in that same period by six dollars in nominal terms, from $510 to $504 weekly. In terms of Latino workers in general and Latina workers more specifically, these declines in nominal income have meant that any increase in prices cuts their real incomes. While these cuts may seem small, they often make a critical difference for people already living with deficit incomes. These pay cuts and price increases may make the difference as to what is on the dinner table and whether necessary medicine can be bought, for example.

The official poverty line is $23,000 for a family of four, a figure that would be better described as extreme poverty. If we use $34,000 annually (or 1.5 times the poverty line) for a family of four, as many governmental and community agencies do when calculating eligibility for different types of aid, poverty among Latinas/os ascends to 21.7 million people, or 42 percent of the Latino population. This is the most severe crisis in living memory for Latina/o workers. As well, disproportionately high numbers of this population are excluded from health care and welfare, lack stable employment or decent housing and find themselves pauperized and persecuted. As of early 2010, one-in-three Latina/os — over fifteen million people — in the United States is poor.

The development of the crisis is, of course, unevenly distributed among different cities and regions. Areas with large Latina/o populations had much higher unemployment rates than the average of their states. This was the case for the border corridor of Texas with Mexico, from Brownsville to El Paso, during the first quarter of 2010. In areas of California with a strong Latina/o presence, the economic recession, according to the BLS, pushed the unemployment rate in the metropolitan areas of Merced or the El Centro above 20 percent. In the metropolitan area of El Centro, near the border of the city of Mexicali, the unemployment rate in March 2010 reached 27 percent of the civilian labour force. At the same time, Boston had an unemployment rate of 8.3 percent, and Detroit had 15 percent. But even in these cities with lower rates of unemployment, if you disaggregate the figures, the rates among African Americans and Latina/os are at the level of the Great Depression of the 1930s.

The extreme poverty and racism that undocumented workers have been enduring has now spread to large sectors of the rest of the Latino population. It is this increasingly common situation of poverty that has united Latinos, with or without documents, and gave the immigrant rights protests of 2006 and 2010 a radical character. These grand mobilizations demanded real citizenship for all, that is, the social rights of citizens to jobs, health care and education — the very rights that the corporate assault has been taking away from citizens as well as denying to non-documented immigrants. The corporate offensive has created a new, emptied-out concept of citizenship, one without elementary social and economic rights. For these reasons, the rebellion against the anti-immigrant legislation has the potential to converge with the needs and demands of all of the poor and working people in the United States.

Migration has not only helped the migrants survive but it has been crucial for the survival of their home communities. Remittances have played a vital role for their families, communities and Mexico's economy. Remittances by Latin American immigrants in the United States grew from $23 billion in 2000 to $70 billion in 2008, an annual rate of 15 percent (Banco de México 2011: 15, 121). But the crisis has changed this dramatically.

The growth of migration from Central America has been dizzying. Long-term poverty, exploitation and repression were important factors in this increased movement, and the revolutionary uprisings and the counter-revolutionary wars carried out by local elites and the United States in the 1980s dramatically escalated the emigration from Central America. The human costs of this traumatic migration have been great, but those who migrated were able to help their families and communities back home through remittances. The growth of remittances to Central America was remarkable. Remittances from Guatemalans in the United States grew annually by an average of 23.8 percent in the 2000–8 period, from an annual amount of $908 million to over $5 billion. The remittances of Mexican workers were the highest. They rose from slightly under $7 billion in 2000 to $26 billion in 2008. This increase of remittances represented a dramatic increase in the income of the poorest 30 percent of the Mexican population (Banco de México 2011: 15, 121). Remittances have played a fundamental part in the reproduction of the labour force in Mexico. The Mexican government itself has recognized the role of remittances in mitigating hunger in entire regions of the country. The Consejo Nacional para la Evaluación de la Política Social (CONEVAL, National Council for the Evaluation of Social Development Policy) made the following estimation at the end of 2008:

If in 2006 there had not been the flow of remittances in the country, 15.9 percent of the total population of the country would have suffered from food insecurity, that is to say, an additional 2 percentage points more — 2.3 million people — above the numbers recorded, according to the Evaluación de la Política de Desarrollo Social en México (Evaluation of Social Development Policy in Mexico). Although all poor families did not receive these resources, these resources contributed to attenuating misery. The document elaborated by the Consejo Nacional de Evaluación de la Política de Desarrollo Social (CONEVAL) details that the remittances that Mexican migrants sent from the United States had grown 405.5 percent in families in food poverty in rural areas between 1992 and 2006. (Informe Ejecutivo para el Diagnóstico del Plan Nacional de Desarrollo, Consejo para la Evaluación de la Política Social, Poder Ejecutivo Federal, México: 2008: 3, 5, authors' translation)

There was a sharp drop in remittances from $26 billion U.S. in 2007 to slightly more than $21 billion U.S. in 2009, a decline of nearly 20 percent. Remittances made a modest recovery in 2010 and 2011, but remain on average 13 percent less than at the height of employment of Mexican migrants in the United States during 2007.

The sharpest drops in remittances have been to those Mexican states where mass migration is of more recent origin. Remittances to Chiapas, for example, fell almost 25 percent from 2008 to 2009. As well, Tabasco, Veracruz, Oaxaca and Yucatán share with Chiapas this especially precipitous drop in remittances as compared to regions of more longstanding emigration. These more recent immigrants to the U.S. labour market are generally in more vulnerable positions, and the decline in remittances is, of course, tied to the sharp deterioration of opportunities for Mexican and Latina/o migrants in the U.S. labour market.

The mass migration of Mexicans northward reflects the failure of the neo-liberal project. Mexico has only been creating 12 percent of the new jobs that would be required to give employment to the two million youths that enter the labour force annually. Only 1.2 million new jobs were created in the nine years from 2001–9 while twenty million young people entered the labour force in the last decade. Though these figures would have been modified, taking into account existing jobs that became available through retirement as well as jobs that disappeared because of business failures and restructuring, these modifications would not change the general picture of the failure of the Mexican economy to create anywhere near an adequate supply of new jobs. Every day, around 6,000 young people enter the labour market while only 720 new jobs are opened up. The neo-liberal project combined with continental integration has made Mexico the third leading exporter of people in the world, following the much more populous countries of China and India (United Nations Population Fund 2011: 69). Remittances are a good indicator of the fall of the income of Mexican workers in the United States, a fall that has been a result of both unemployment and declining real salaries. Both remittances and migration have slowed down, but the reverse migration predicted by some has not come about for several reasons. First of all, there are no jobs to return to in Mexico. Secondly, tighter border security, while not stopping immigration, has made it more risky and more expensive and is a deterrent to returning to Mexico to wait out the U.S. downturn. Finally, vast numbers of Mexican families now have a transnational family income that depends on employment in and remittances from the United States. This has led to impoverished Mexican families sending money north so their immigrant relatives can bide time for the hoped-for recovery of jobs (Lacey 2009).

Mass Immigration: Safety Valve for Mexican Capitalism, Subsidy for U.S. Capitalism

The mass migration of Mexicans to the U.S relieves some of the pressure on Mexican capitalism to provide jobs for the rapidly growing labour force. It also serves as a safety valve for discontent as those leaving are often the most dynamic young people in the working class, people who have been or have the potential to be, rank-and-file leaders of social struggles. However, their experiences of greater opportunities and a higher standard of living in the United States, even below the U.S. poverty line, may give them a more critical perspective on the extreme deprivation that their families and communities suffer in Mexico, a perspective that may be transmitted to their home communities through family, friendship or community ties. And the remittances sent home by immigrant workers alleviate the extreme poverty of many families and communities.

The mass immigration from Mexico and elsewhere plays an important role in subsidizing U.S. society in at least two ways. Mexican society pays the costs of reproduction of a significant portion of the U.S. labour force. The families, societies and governments of the immigrants' home countries pay the costs of raising, schooling and training kids, and, when they arrive at working age, a significant portion of them join the U.S. labour force. The fiscal savings thereby experienced by the United States are paid for by Mexico's social expenditures. This subsidization by Mexico is an invisible but massive transfer of social wealth from Mexico to the United States. The "demographic bonus," the growth of the working age population relative to the total population, is collected by U.S. businessmen in U.S. territory as well as in the *maquila* zones.

The second important contribution that immigrants make to U.S. public finances is their contribution to the pension and medical assistance programs, known as Social Security. The 1986 immigration reform law made it obligatory for all employers to ask their employees for their official Social Security card. Undocumented workers, therefore, had to resort to the emerging black market in fake Social Security cards to satisfy this condition of employment. The employer would then fill out a W2 form with the social security number of the employee and deduct 12.4 percent for Social Security and 2.9 percent for Medicaid from their gross wages. For example, $2,450 would be deducted from an income of $25,000 for these payments. For an average North American making contributions now, after 35 years of work, this would represent a retirement income of $1,200 per month.

The great majority of undocumented workers have to present a false Social Security card in order to work. While they will make significant contributions to Social Security over their working life, they will never receive any benefits from it. The Social Security administration itself recognizes the existence of millions of people who pay into Social Security through false registrations. In fact, undocumented workers using false Social Security cards contribute billions of dollars to the Social Security Administration and will never receive a cent back (Lantigua 2011; Leland 2006; Porter 2005).

The crisis and the new wave of neo-liberal reforms and cutbacks continue to push Mexicans northward. And, in the United States, these continuing policies have meant that recent waves of Mexican immigrants are entering a labour market that continues to be downgraded. The combination of the increasing numbers of desperate migrants and a general downward push in the U.S. labor market have created conditions for scapegoating immigrants. In previous crises in the United States, immigrants were scapegoated, racial profiling was widely used and massive numbers of immigrants were deported. Racist attacks against immigrants had already been developing strongly before this recent crisis.

The ongoing tension between the labour recruitment and regulation strategy of sections of capital and the opposition of various sectors of society to the inclusion of the bearers of this labour power as fellow members of society is intensifying. As Michael Kearney has put it, "Foreign labor is desired, but the person in whom it is embodied is not desired" (cited in Peck 1996: 10).

Conflicts over status and citizenship rights become confounded with conflict over real or perceived economic interests. These issues are used as mobilizing issues in political struggles (e.g., Buchanan in the presidential primaries of 1996 and 2000 and also the anti-immigrant Bill 187 in California) building on the status and the cultural and economic anxieties of sections of the American population. Five states — Georgia, Alabama, South Carolina,

Indiana and Utah — passed anti-immigrant laws in early 2011 modelled on Arizona's SB 1070. The implementation of most of the provisions of these laws has been blocked by federal judges, but Arizona has appealed these decisions to the conservative federal Supreme Court (New America Media 2012). There is a complex political battle between powerful sectors of U.S. business who want immigrant workers, xenophobic right-wingers who do not want non-white immigrants at all, workers fearful of "unfair" competition and those fighting for full civil rights for immigrant workers and their families. The challenge for the workers' movement is to build a culture and politics of solidarity that can overcome the deliberately fostered competition and hostility within the working class. A culture and politics of working-class solidarity requires combining anti-racism and a transformatory program with an economy in which there would be decent jobs for all.

Notes

1. Nine million people obtained permanent residence in the U.S. through legal processes in the period from 1991–2000 (U.S. Census Bureau, Statistical Abstract of the United States: 2012, Table 23, Page Population 31). 4.3 million, or 47 percent, of these new permanent residents came from Latin America. The percentage of Latin Americans that received legal resident status increased to 55 percent from 2000 to 2007. Four million of the 7.2 million people that received legal residency in this period were from Latin America. In addition to the 600,000 new legal residents that arrived from Latin America annually in this latter period, another three million non-authorized Latin American immigrants also came.

Chapter 6

Continental Integration
from Below
The History of Transnational Labour Markets
and Labour Movements in North America

Historically, there have been two very different processes of cross-border labour integration in North America. In the case of Canada and the United States, there is a long history of workers in both countries being members of transnational unions (so-called international unions). In the case of Mexico and the United States, there has been a long history of Mexico serving as a reserve army of labour for the U.S. economy and the limited integration of Mexican workers into labour unions within the United States.

Both Canada and Mexico have long had significant degrees of economic integration with the United States, though few links with each other directly. This integration has taken a number of forms, although export and investment are two of the most well known. But there has also been a significant degree of labour market integration between the two sets of countries and a remarkable degree of trade union integration between Canada and the United States. These relations did not start with CUFTA or NAFTA. They have a long history, but have undergone important changes over time. The free trade agreement between Canada and the United States preceded NAFTA by five years. The initiative for CUFTA, as discussed in Chapter 2, came from Canadian business. The free trade agreement, from the point of view of Canadian business, was seen as an instrument to promote industrial restructuring through trade policy as well as to keep the U.S. open for Canadian goods and investment. As wage levels and associated costs were not that disparate, and, in fact, Canadian social benefits were and are, in general, superior to those in the United States, U.S. labour did not feel threatened by an economic agreement. Access to Canadian resources was also a very important element in the positive response of U.S. business and the state to a trade agreement.

Canada has been more a receiving than a sending country of immigrants. And in those periods when there was significant emigration from Canada to the United States, Canadians were received and assimilated into the white stream of "racial" formation. Canadians entered the north and west of the United States where state labour regulation tended to be less repressive and

87

where wages were higher than in the more labour-repressive southwest, which is historically the entry point for most new waves of Mexican immigrants and the centuries-old residence of many Mexicans from before the U.S annexation of much of northern Mexico in the mid-nineteenth century.

Labour market concerns, however, were central to U.S. business in the case of NAFTA. Various waves of Mexican workers had been incorporated into U.S. industry through immigration and expelled repeatedly in Mexican–U.S. history. But the development of the Border Industrialization Program (BIP) in the late 1960s, later to become the *maquila* industry, created the institutional framework within which Mexican labour could be used within Mexico in a U.S. corporate-controlled transnational production system. The BIP developed out of a number of related concerns. The Mexican government was concerned about the rise of unemployment with the ending of the Bracero Program in 1964 while U.S. manufacturers were concerned about lowering costs of production to compete with Japanese and European companies. Many U.S. companies (as well as Japanese and European companies) were already engaged in some shared production or contracting out of production to cheap labour areas in Asia, Puerto Rico and Haiti. Items 806.30 and 807 of the *U.S. Tariff Schedule* facilitated partial production abroad. When the goods were shipped back to the U.S. market, duty would only be charged on the value added. Thus, duty could be minimal as the value-added would be very low due to low wages, low overhead and transfer pricing. Mexico's common border with the United States and short transportation distances were key advantages over Asia. In addition to reduced costs on the part of manufacturers, major retailers wanted to label products as "Made in the U.S." Sears, the major retail chain in the United States, provides a good example of this aspect. Sears became concerned that so much of its merchandise had foreign labels. Thus, Sears pushed its suppliers to relocate to Mexico and take advantage of the BIP. Sears suppliers could now compete with Asian suppliers and Sears could label its products as "Made in America" (Sklair 1989: 50–52).

This was a crucial step in the deepening integration of the Mexican labour force into the U.S. labour market from the other side of the border. Both the development of *maquilas* and the expansion of informal immigration involved the incorporation of the Mexican labour force into U.S. production under conditions and terms that were far inferior to those of other workers in the United States. A central, but not exclusive, purpose of NAFTA was to institutionalize neo-liberal labour market relations by treaty. The fear of accelerated plant relocation and job flight that this prospect produced was the reason that U.S. and Canadian unions opposed NAFTA.

Pre-NAFTA Labour Markets

There are a number of important dimensions that shape the formation of the different labour market situations between the two sets of countries: 1) the timing and mode of entry into the new country, 2) the social, political and economic character of region of settlement, 3) the occupational and skill characteristics of the immigrants and 4) the role of racialist categorization and racism as mediating factors in processes of integration or segregation in the new country.

The formation of ethnic or "racial" consciousness and cleavages has to be seen as a socially produced process. Ethnic and racial categorization is a part of social processes that involve relations of power, exploitation and resistance. This does not make them less real in the lives of people. But it is important to recognize the social and historical character of these categorizations and the fact that they change over time in the course of co-operation and struggle within and between groups. "Ethnogenesis" refers to processes by which ethnic and "racial" groups are formed with changing boundaries of inclusion and exclusion.

The British origins of many of the early immigrant workers to both the United States and Canada facilitated a common identity among them. And common histories and identifications within trades in the home country also contributed to this development. This shared background of the Anglo immigrants facilitated the forging of a partially common Canadian–U.S. labour market in some periods. Thus, the Canadian–U.S. labour relationship has for some time had strong aspects of a regional, rather than an international, integration. This is typified in the development of Canadian unionism as a regional sector of U.S. unionism. Later waves of European immigrants were, over time, and not without tensions and conflicts, assimilated into this white stream, whose ethnogenesis was forged in a complex process of inclusion and exclusion (Roediger 1999, 2005). By "white stream," we are referring to the development of various levels and degrees of shared ethnic or "racial" identity amongst different groups of "white" people.

Canadians In the United States

There was large scale immigration of Anglo-Canadians and French-Canadians to the U.S. in the nineteenth century and the first three decades of the twentieth century There was also a large-scale migration of people from the U.S. to Canada in that same period, and a net transfer of 2.8 million Canadians to the U.S. from 1840–1930 (Ramirez 2004: 21). The number of Canadians living in the U.S. went from almost 500,000 in 1870 to one million in 1900, that is, from around 12 percent to 22 percent of the resident population of Canada. And in that same year, 1900, one million people born in the U.S. lived in Canada, one-fifth of the population of Canada (Gabaccia

2004: 41). Canadians were the third most important immigrant group in the U.S. up to the 1930s (Ramirez 2004: 17). There were two main population groups of Canadian immigrants to the U.S., Anglo-Canadians and French-Canadians. Though they were different in significant ways, both would enter the white stream of the U.S., the former more seamlessly, the latter through processes of linguistic and cultural assimilation similar to that experienced by non-English speaking, white European immigrants.

Though there was this great flow of population back and forth between the United States and Canada at various times in the nineteenth and early twentieth centuries, no distinctly American communities developed in Canada or distinctly Canadian communities in the United States, with the exception of French-Canadian ones (Zunz and Widdis, both cited by Ramirez 2001: 69). Anglo-Canadians in the U.S. often came with high levels of skill and were likely to be high up on the occupational ladder. The invisibility of these Anglo-Canadians in popular consciousness as well as in academic studies would seem to reflect their seamless amalgamation into U.S. society as fellow Anglo whites (Ramirez 2001: 62; Gabaccia 2004).

These "invisible immigrants" do not seem to have seen themselves — and to have been seen — as different people but as fragments of a common people. There was an integration, or, as one Canadian author put it, a "mingling" of people (Hansen 1940). Other immigrant groups, including the French-Canadian, would come to be incorporated into Anglo dominance, whether within the ideological trappings of the melting pot ideology of the United States or that of the Canadian mosaic.

French-Canadian immigrants, soon to become Franco-Americans, unlike the Anglo-Canadian immigrants, have received a considerable amount of academic examination even though their numbers were comparable. The Anglo-Canadians were not as visible or different and, given the tendency of immigration studies to focus on the assimilation of culturally different people by their new society, have been generally ignored (Gabaccia 2004; Ramirez 2001, 2004). The French-Canadian migrants, however, were linguistically and culturally different than the Anglo-Americans. They were generally less skilled and lower on the occupational ladder than their Anglo-Canadian counterparts. French-Canadian migrants had experienced institutionalized discrimination within Canadian society. For example, English was the working language of the railway system and railway centres in Montreal — as it was in Mexico until 1907 — though most of the population spoke French. Skilled jobs were held by English-speaking workers and those who spoke French held the less-skilled jobs. The French-Canadian migration to the U.S. was to the textile mills of the New England states, where they formed distinctive communities, given their linguistic differences and their continuing links to and contiguity with Quebec. But they were treated as whites. They, in fact, seemed to have faced less vicious discrimination than the Italian immigrants in both Canada and the United States (Ramirez 1991). While the Anglo-Canadians disappeared into the Anglo-American population, the French-Canadian immigrants went through processes of assimilation to a white American identity as other European immigrants, with more or less difficulty, would (Gerstle 1989).

White European immigrants to the United States often faced severe prejudice, discrimination and ethnic stereotyping (e.g., the Irish and Italians) but over time became part of the United States or Canadian white stream. Ethnic categories are socially created and involve ongoing processes of setting the boundaries of inclusion and exclusion. The ethnogenesis of white identity in the United States involved struggles to overcome racist attitudes towards certain groups (Southern Europeans, Irish) and maintain other groups as non-white. While there is prejudice, hierarchy and discrimination within the white stream, there is a relative inclusiveness in the differentiation from the non-white groups. Part of the process of the ethnogenesis of the dominant "racial" group is the development of a sense of shared reputability and inclusion as good and worthwhile "Americans" or "Canadians." These ethnic and class categories relate in important ways to labour market segmentation as they involve networks of inclusion and exclusion into various labour market niches.

Mexicans In the United States

Mexican entry and incorporation into the United States was, however, very different than that of Canadian and European immigrants. Initial entry, in the mid-nineteenth century, was through the U.S. conquest of what was northern Mexico at that time. The nature of this initial contact between the "Anglos" or "Americans" and the Mexicans would come to be crucial in the development of a colonized and racialized form of ethnic subordination.

The northern regions of Mexico were sparsely populated and, prior to railway development in the last decades of the nineteenth century, were poorly connected to central Mexico. There was neither a strong national identity among the Mexicans of these northern regions nor a strong, shared identity amongst them. The large landowners thought of themselves as Spanish/European and racially different and superior to the *mestizos* (mixed populations) and indigenous peoples of the regions. Many of the small landowning settlers, the *rancheros*, were *mestizo*. There were many armed conflicts between the large "Spanish" landowners, the *mestizo rancheros* and the settlers arriving from the U.S. on the one hand and Indigenous peoples on the other. Indigenous peoples resisted land takeovers and displacement from traditional common grounds. The Anglo settler population of Texas led a successful rebellion for independence from Mexico in 1836, and

Texas became an independent republic. In 1846, the United States went to war with Mexico ostensibly over a boundary dispute between Texas and Mexico. The U.S. defeated Mexico and incorporated over half of Mexico's territory (the present U.S. southwest and California) in the peace treaty signed in 1848.

Mexico, including these northern regions, was a racially stratified society where class position was very intertwined with and, in fact, often shaped claims to ethnic status. Those who would become Mexican-Americans were divided on the basis of class and race. The landed Spanish/European elite both sought acceptance, and for a period received it, as fellow whites, from the Anglo-Americans. The people of mixed origin, the *mestizos*, which included Indigenous people who had left their original communities and assimilated to the *mestizo* cultures of mining camps, ranches and towns were generally viewed in an extremely racist manner by both the Anglo-Americans and the Mexican elites. This divided Mexican population would, over time, experience more and more common subjugation and in its resistance, would forge itself into a common identity, as happened with the African slave population. But this forging, this ethnogenesis, over time, of a common Mexican-American identity, would be a terrain of contestation both within the different layers of the Mexican population and between the Mexican population and the Anglo community. These struggles and processes of labelling and the development of group consciousness would change over time in relation to processes of capitalist development in the U.S. southwest as well as in relation to developments in both the United States and Mexico. There was a frequent tension between the original Mexicans in the area and various layers of later Mexican immigrants.

The formal U.S. citizenship rights granted to the conquered Mexican population came to be more and more denied in practice through a variety of mechanisms that included violent, state-executed or tolerated repression, segregation and the denial of voting rights (Barton 2004: 157). From the period prior to Texas independence up until the 1870s, there had been a friendly coexistence between the Anglo-American newcomers and the old Mexican elites. The situation changed with the capitalist development of agriculture and a large-scale enclosure movement that expropriated the property of the large Mexican landowners as well as small and medium-size *rancheros* (ranchers and farmers). This displaced the landed elites from their land and their basis of power and status, and also destroyed the economic bases of the *rancheros* and their communities. This was a process of colonial "primitive accumulation" that became melded with the pre-existing racism (Montejano 1987). The Mexican population in the conquered territories was transformed from a population with significant social class heterogeneity to one that was more homogeneous. Most Mexicans in the conquered areas came to be landless and concentrated in the lowest paying jobs. Montejano cites a study of south and west Texas by Arnoldo De León that shows this compression of Mexican social stratification from 1850 to 1900:

> At mid-century, the rural Mexican population was equally divided in thirds among ranch-farm owners (34 percent), skilled labourers (29 percent) and manual labourers (34 percent). By the turn of the century, the two top tiers had shrunk — ranch-farm owners comprised 16 percent of the Texas Mexican population, skilled labourers 12 percent — and the bottom tier of manual labourers had expanded, comprising 67 percent, or two of every three adult Mexicans. In contrast, the segment of the Anglo-American population that showed the greatest increase in the nineteenth century was the ranch-farm owning class, from 2 percent in 1850 to 31 percent by 1900. (Montejano 1987: 73)

The developments in Texas were not unique, according to Josef Barton:

> The Southwest proved to be the great equalizer. At whatever stage in the transition [to capitalist agriculture] the Mexicans arrived, the new organization of work homogenized them into landless workers, harnessed to the most advanced agrarian capitalism in the world, and denied them even rights as persons through the operations of the state. (Barton 2004: 157)

An internal colonial model developed and was consolidated by a variety of institutional mechanisms including segregated schools and the denial of voting rights, similar to what happened to African Americans in the U.S. south. State force and popular vigilantism were used to enforce the colonized character of the Mexican population and its availability as a cheap labour force. The Texas Rangers, formed as a military unit in 1835 in the fight to secede from Mexico, became a paramilitary state police force used against Indigenous peoples and Mexicans fighting the Anglo conquest. The Texas Rangers were disbanded by the U.S. federal government after the U.S. Civil War — Texas had been part of the secessionist south — but it was reconstituted as a state police force in 1874 by the Texas Legislature:

> In South Texas, *Tejanos* [Texas Mexicans] lost their land through fraud and coercion. Texas Rangers' hatred and brutality toward the Mexicans was extreme; the Rangers acted as hired guns to Anglo-Texan ranchers who dispossessed and proletarianized *Tejano* ranchers and *vaqueros* [cowboys]. The eventual violent collapse of *Tejano* ranching society took place in the early twentieth century, when the Texas

Rangers, intermediaries in the transition to capitalism, cleaned out the remaining *Tejano* landowners, summarily executing more than three hundred "suspected Mexicans." (Vargas 2011: 170)

As later waves of Mexican migrants arrived through a border that remained open, they would be incorporated into this structure of internal colonialism, state violence and institutionalized racism. The newly arriving Mexicans became part of a vast aggregate of cheap labour that was labelled and treated as racially inferior:

> In the long run, then, southwestern [Anglo-American] capitalists solidified class solidarity through politics. They engineered court-house coups in order to guarantee control of local governments. On the state level, their machines controlled the settled Mexican population and excluded the newcomers. They struck crucial close alliances with rural police, sheriffs' deputies in small towns, troops of Texas Rangers, and officials of the United States Immigration and Naturalization Service. All these constituted mobile forces which landlords deployed against local uprisings in the 1890s, insurrectionary movements during the Mexican Revolution, and the union movement of the 1930s. (Barton 2004: 157)

State governments, as well as the federal government, have played an important role in controlling Mexican labour in the U.S. The U.S. state has played a central role in controlling the ebb and flow of Mexican labour into the United States and back to Mexico through active recruitment campaigns and mass deportations. But it is important to avoid reductionist views of the role of the state in this process. While the labour needs of particular capitalist interests were a central concern, there was an ongoing struggle between these capitalists and restrictionist and racist U.S. politicians, communities and trade unions. The ebb and flow of these struggles, the labour supply situation and the dynamics of U.S. politics would shape the nature of Mexican labour recruitment and expulsion.

The Mexican-American population has been subject to a regime of internal colonialism, institutionalized racism and extreme exploitation. Social control was maintained by a combination of coercion and racist ideology that fostered cohesion among whites and exclusion of Mexicans. Law, labour market manipulation and coercion by both the state and vigilante groups were used to keep Mexicans in super-exploited segments of the labour market, initially in rural areas and later, with more indirect methods of control, in urban areas. The African-American population, though with a different entry point, has gone through similar processes. The collective identities of both Mexican-Americans and African-Americans have been forged in the cauldron of severe, shared oppression and resistance, both open and subterranean, to that oppression.

Pre-NAFTA Labour Movements

The historical and current relationship of unions between Mexico, Canada and the United States reflects the differences that have been discussed above. Canadian and U.S. workers were and are often members of the same unions; Canadian workers belonged to districts or regions of what are called "international" unions, but were simply U.S.–Canada unions. The Mexican case is very different.

Canada

Canada is unique in the world in that much of its labour movement has been — and continues to be — part of U.S.-based and U.S.-dominated international unions. The United Steel Workers (USW), for example, has several Canadian districts organized by region, but their international headquarters is in Pittsburgh. Until 1985, the United Auto Workers (UAW) was structured in the same manner, with its international headquarters in Detroit. And many unions like the Labourers International Union of North America (LIUNA) were and continue to be U.S.–Canadian unions. This is a good indicator that U.S. union leaders and members consider their Canadian brothers and sisters to be worthy of membership, of union "citizenship," in the same unions. Attempts by Canadian sections of international unions to split off — motivated by Canadian nationalism, discontent with union head offices and disagreements about union strategy — have generally been strongly and successfully resisted; the primary example of successful separation is the formation of the Canadian Auto Workers (CAW), which split off from the UAW in 1984.

British skilled workers who had migrated to both countries started some of the early American Federation of Labor (AFL) craft unions as common Canadian–U.S. unions (Heron 1996: 33; Crispo 1967: 13–14). Canadians were welcomed into the various railway brotherhoods and craft unions of the United States. Common union membership facilitated labour mobility between the two countries, and this trans-border character of certain sectors of the labour market and of union membership itself fostered cross-border solidarities within particular ethnic groups and craft groups.

Mexico

We find a completely different pattern in the case of Mexico. The U.S. railway brotherhoods, for example, did organize skilled rail workers in Mexico, but only those who were American and British. English was the working language of Mexico's railways until 1907, when the Diaz dictatorship "Mexicanized" the railways. Mexicans — in Mexico — had been formally excluded from the skilled railway brotherhoods and relegated to the less-skilled jobs. Mexicans and Mexican-Americans in both Mexico and the United States were excluded from these railway unions — as were African Americans — whereas Canadian whites were welcomed.

The attitude of the AFL was long one of restricting immigration and excluding Mexicans (whether they were U.S. citizens or immigrants from Mexico) from U.S. unions. Thus, for much of the twentieth century, many U.S. unions excluded Mexican-Americans and African Americans either through formal statutes or by informal practices. And, today, the relations between Mexican and U.S. unions are international, whereas many unions north of the Mexican border are joint Canadian and American.[1]

Note

1. While these are some of the key differences in the historical formation of the two sets of cross-border labour markets and labour movements, there are other important elements. A more complete comparison should include the great differences in the historical development of the Mexican and Canadian economies, the different degrees and modes of integration of these economies with the U.S. economy in different periods as well as differing demographic characteristics, including the nature and levels of immigration, population growth and age structures.

PART III

WORKERS AND UNIONS

Responses and
Continental Integration
from Below

Chapter 7

Fighting Back
Workers, Unions and Continental Solidarity

Solidarity or Competition
in the Context of Uneven Development

An effective fightback against the continental capitalist offensive requires working-class responses that include but go beyond the local, regional and national. The fightback has also to be continental. Strategies that promote greater solidarity between unions, between unionized and non-unionized workers and across national borders have to be developed. There are both encouraging prospects as well as serious obstacles to the development of such solidarity. The contiguity of the three countries, the deepening integration of continental production chains and the significant and growing presence of the Mexican working class in the United States gives strategic significance to this continental focus. Some of these characteristics also apply to Central America and the Caribbean as well as to faraway places, such as China. Many of our arguments for continental labour solidarity can be extended as propositions that may need qualification for various areas with differing forms and degrees of integration with North America. And there are other aspects of labour solidarity that are not as closely related to union struggles, such as the struggle for democracy, the opposition to war and the defence of self-determination for Indigenous peoples, that go beyond the scope of this book.

Capitalism pits individual workers and different labouring populations against each other in the search for jobs. This competitive struggle for jobs creates strong obstacles to the solidarity needed for workers to mount an effective fightback against the power of capital. Capitalism promotes a culture of competition among workers, and between workers at separate workplaces, to undermine collective worker resistance. Capitalism also takes advantage of pre-existing differences and tensions between groups (such as ethnicity, nationality, gender, domestic-born versus immigrant, among other differences) to enhance the typical and time-worn capitalist strategy of divide and rule. This strategy has always been an important part of capitalism. There is, however, an important difference between gender disparities and other disparities within the working class as gender differences are present within the working class family itself. Women generally receive lower wages than men, even for doing equivalent jobs. Women are also generally concentrated in lower-wage sectors of the labour market through the sexist practices of employers. As well, those who are cohabiting or married bear the double-duty of both wage and domestic labour or depend on the male breadwinner. The divisions within the male working class between those who are relatively anchored in the work force, those who are primarily in the reserve army of labour and those who are floating between the two sectors are replicated among women, though with greater proportions in the latter two categories. Women in the especially disadvantaged segments of the working class, especially visible minorities or immigrant women, are among the most poor, precarious and marginalized members of the working class

The fact that gender differences and gender inequality are present within the vast majority of heterosexual families gives the complexity of gender, as compared to ethnicity, race, ability or other differences within the working class, a unique character. Working-class men and women are intimate family partners at home with a division of labour that is, by and large, patriarchal. That is, the relation within the home tends to be one of male dominance, with women primarily responsible for raising the family. Male workers and male-dominated unions have frequently acted to maintain a sexist division of labour in the family as well as in the labour market. These practices by male workers and male-dominated unions have to be understood as part of the complex framework of the institutionalized sexism of patriarchal capitalist societies.

Patriarchy was not an invention of capitalists. It was inherited from previous social formations and has been used by capitalists to create or reinforce divisions and competition within the working class. Though women bear the brunt of gender inequality, the costs to men are also significant. Gender domination, while involving privileges, also involves significant costs for men. It obstructs the full development of the potential of their partners and of the relationship itself. The material and status gains for working-class men come in the context of their own subordination within capitalist society, a subordination that often robs them of dignity and control as the power of capitalists shapes their daily life and their opportunities. The sense of powerlessness that all workers experience in capitalist society may be disguised by the male breadwinner role, but that role itself is increasingly being destroyed by the neo-liberal offensive against the working class. But the destruction of the male breadwinner and the greater presence of women in the labour market has not eroded the patriarchal household structure nor raised working-class women to economic independence. Rather, it has undermined the fragile dignity of the male breadwinner while intensifying the double day for women. The race to the bottom cannot be the context for the emancipation of women from patriarchy and exploitation. The challenge to patriarchy, powerlessness and exploitation has to involve the transformation of the family as part of the transformation of working-class culture, a transformation necessary to build the solidarity necessary to fight back against the big business offensive.

Sexist practices within the working class — in the household, in the labour market, at the job site, and in unions — are important barriers to working-class solidarity. A new working-class practice and culture of solidarity requires an attack on patriarchal practices within society as well as within the working class itself. The self-organization of women within unions and within the labour movement is necessary to pressure unions to transform themselves into organizations fighting for fundamental cultural change in gender relations. These struggles, as well as those against racism and anti-immigrant attitudes and practices in the working class, are a necessary part of labour's transformation, though they often lead, in the short run, to tensions within working-class organizations. These struggles and tensions are a necessary part of the struggle for an inclusive working-class culture of solidarity.

The massive increase in women's participation in the labour market and the push of the feminist movement in the 1970s and 1980s in Canada and the United States to open up more segments of the labour market to women roughly coincided with the deliberate degradation and union-busting of the neo-liberal offensive. More and more "good" working-class jobs became low wage and precarious at the same time that more and more women were pushed into the labour market by declining wages (Fudge and Vosko 2003: 183–209, especially 197, 202–4). More and more wives had to enter the labour market to try to keep up the family's standard of living.

Sexism has been an important tool in the downgrading of jobs and workers rights in North America through the *maquila* program. The *maquila* program started as a legal regime of exemption from tariffs along with other privileges for plants in northern Mexico as part of a continental production process. The program soon became a blueprint for a more general process of the downward restructuring of the labour market that has become widespread in Mexico. The downgrading of the labour market through the *maquila* programme was gender-based as well as geographically based. Young, single women were the employees of choice, even though the initial government rationale for the Border Industrialization Program, the predecessor to *maquilas*, was to replace jobs lost by men when the Bracero Program (discussed in Chapter 5) ended. Very few men were hired in the first phase of *maquila* development in northern Mexico. Young, single women, often new to the labour force and to the locations of these new plants, were thought to be more pliable and less apt to resist intensified exploitation. The workforce was feminized, both in the sense that its composition became more female and that the jobs themselves were downgraded. Plant relocation did not only take place from Canada and the U.S. to Mexico, plants also moved from central Mexico to the *maquila* zones with the same goal of increasing managerial autocracy and lowering wages. The super-exploitative labour regime of *maquilas* has now become the model for the restructuring of labour relations throughout Mexico (Healy 2008: 151–57).

During the long post-World War II period of economic expansion (the Fordist/Keynesian era) in the United States and Canada, and during the import substitution industrialization period in Mexico, workers in oligopolistic sectors were able to insulate themselves from the general competition and make some very important gains in terms of wages, benefits and working conditions. These forms of sectoral labour solidarity (mainly seen within particular craft and industrial unions, and at times the union movement as a whole) always left out major sectors of the working class. Their exclusion was not simply the result of the sectoral focus of unions but also of the aggressive resistance to unionization by capital and the state, particularly in the competitive sectors of the economy.

Labour solidarity, while rooted in the relationship of workers to capitalists, emerges in the course of association and shared struggle (Fantasia 1988). Labour solidarity has to be seen as a cultural and political concept as much, or even more, than an economic one. It can have varied specific contents and organizational forms, and its boundaries can be more widely or more narrowly drawn. Craft unions, as the guilds that preceded them, expressed and developed solidarity among certain skilled occupations. Industrial unions organized and helped create fraternal sentiments among workers, both skilled and unskilled, in specific industries. General unions, such as the IWW (Industrial Workers of the World) and the Casa del Obrero Mundial (COM, House of the World Worker), sought to develop solidarity among the whole of the working class, as did socialist, anarchist and communist labour movements. The concept of international solidarity does not differ in principle from the concept of solidarity within the working class of one local community, one region or one nation, expressing itself at various times within the bounds of certain crafts or industries, or, at times, expressing itself class-wide. The process of developing international solidarity is necessarily more complex and difficult for a variety of reasons. Different national working classes exist under different industrial relations regimes, are often linked to national political parties in different systems and may also have language and cultural barriers as well as international antagonisms. Great differences in incomes and working conditions between working classes in countries whose economic development is very unequal also creates much greater complexity for the development of international solidarity.

The extension of North American continental production systems to include Mexico enhances the possibilities of using competition between workers in the three countries as a tool of labour control. Both the threat and practice of relocation, along with the increasing casualization of the labour force, have been part of an intertwined, dual strategy that has transformed the conditions of work in all three NAFTA countries, thereby increasing managerial power. The casualization of labour fragments the working class and obscures their common situation. Sub-contracting, hiring workers through temporary employment agencies, dividing workplaces between casual and permanent and other devices all seek to undermine the basis of collective resistance that previously existed in workplaces with a relatively stable labour force. This assault on workers' rights, wages and working and living conditions did not start with NAFTA, but NAFTA deepened, widened and gave international treaty support to these neo-liberal practices. While neo-liberalism and NAFTA are aimed at reducing labour costs and increasing labour discipline and productivity, the use of the threat or practice of relocation as a tool of capital to discipline workers is not new nor is it unique to cross-border or international situations (Cowie 1999; Bronfenbrenner 1997).

The extremely uneven development of North America poses a great obstacle to a continental fightback even though all three working classes are under a similar and related attack. Differences in culture, language, national traditions, industrial relations regimes and standards of wages and working conditions make solidarity more complex and difficult, but they by no means preclude it. Canadian workers have built a labour movement within Canada that is binational (Quebec and the rest of Canada) and bilingual (French-English) and has incorporated immigrants from all over the world. And the U.S. labour movement — after a long history of anti-immigrant policies and racist exclusion of African Americans, Latina/os and Asians by many unions — has been struggling to develop a more inclusive unionism and has reversed its historic opposition to undocumented immigrant workers. The task of overcoming differences of language, culture and nationality has been a constant one throughout working-class history. The tool of divide and rule has to be overcome by the practice of solidarity.

The developments in the last two decades have intensified and deeply institutionalized the differential and uneven integration of North America. The two different cross-national experiences discussed in Chapter 6 could be building blocks for tri-national unions. The international unions that have joined U.S. and Canadian workers in common organizations demonstrate that national boundaries and different industrial relations regimes do not preclude common organization. Many of these cross-national unions continue to exist (e.g., the United Steelworkers and UNITE HERE!). Many Canadian trade unionists were sharply critical of continental unions for two interconnected reasons: these unions were generally dominated by the much larger U.S. sections and, with few exceptions, these international unions played a conservative, anti-Left role in the long Cold War period, often collaborating with the U.S. government in its imperial interventions. It has not, however, always been the case. This was not true of the IWW in the first two decades of the twentieth century or of the Congress of Industrial Organizations (CIO) in the 1930s and early 1940s.

The Limits of Presently Existing Unionism

The long defensive retreat of unionism cannot be completely attributed to the power of business. Unions have continued to act on the basis of an old framework of labour relations while business was in the midst of transforming that framework. While business fought for class-wide demands and a different vision of capitalism, unions, for the most part, engaged in fragmented union-by-union defensive battles aimed at slowing down, rather than challenging, the corporate offensive in its fundamentals. Unions did not counter the business offensive with class-wide demands and a class-wide alternative vision of society that could have united more of the working class against the business offensive. Unions have often led fights for welfare measures and workers' rights that benefitted all of the working class, and the gains that unions made for their own members often put pressure on non-union employers to raise wages or benefits to avoid unionization. But some of the gains made by stronger unions did not spread to the rest of the working class, a fact exploited by big business in its recurrent divide-and-rule tactics. Members of weaker unions, non-unionized workers, the floating sections of the labour force and the poor who had benefitted little, if at all, from some of the most important gains made by members of the stronger unions didn't identify with these relatively privileged sectors of the working class. While these groups contain many white male workers, women and visible minorities were and continue to be over-represented among them. Existing gender and racial biases facilitated playing off workers against each other, and business used these divisions within the working class to keep it divided. Business first attacked one sector, then another, each time suggesting that the interests of the sector under attack were in conflict with the interests of other sectors of the working class: the "overpaid" private sector workers made "us" uncompetitive, the "lazy" unemployed and welfare recipients undermined "our" work ethic and the "privileged" public sector workers caused the debt crisis of the state. In times of economic expansion as well as in times of economic recession, big business invented arguments to justify the assault on the vast majority of the population.

Unions represent specific groups of workers, and the navigation between fighting for their interests and fighting for the general interests of the class is very difficult, whatever the politics and class perspective of the union. The necessity, at times, of risking, subordinating or even sacrificing short-term sectional interests for broader class interests is a difficult challenge for any union. Workers and unions have fewer resources than capital for sustaining long battles, and workers and unions are subject to devastating fines, if not outright repression, if they violate restraints imposed by the state. The act of extending solidarity even when it conflicts with the immediate interests of a union requires an identification with broader class interests. Yet workers have made these sacrifices time and again, when they've refused to cross picket lines of other workers or to accept jobs as replacement workers in spite of the financial costs and possible legal or employment risks for themselves.

This broader class solidarity has been a strong current in the labour movement in certain periods and was characteristic of the IWW, the Casa del Obrero Mundial and the One Big Union (OBU) in the early twentieth century. This class-wide solidarity was defeated by a combination of state repression, material gains for significant segments of the working class and challenges from sectional, economistic unionism. The winning of private pension and medical plans for some unions and limited welfare benefits for broad sectors of the working class in Canada and the U.S., as well as the gains made by sectors of the working class during the ISI period in Mexico, all played enormous roles in the undermining of these movements. As well, direct state repression and state-facilitated corporate repression have been used repeatedly to defeat class-inclusive, transformatory projects of the working classes of the three countries, such as the IWW (primarily anarcho-syndicalist in orientation) and the socialist currents in the U.S. workers movement in the 1900–1920 period (Kimeldorf 1999). In the case of Mexico, the regime that emerged from the 1910–20 revolution fostered the incorporation of unions into the ruling party and into the project of state-promoted capitalist development.

The defeat of class-inclusive, transformatory unionism was also a consequence of strategic choices made by key unions. Some unions, focusing on short-term gains, made strategic alliances with business and reformist capitalist governments that undermined the political independence of these movements. These strategies often flowed out of a pragmatism of the possible, the notion that you have to constrain your demands to what seems possible within the existing framework, rather than seeking to challenge the limits of that framework. As well, Communist Party activists in each of the three countries played important roles in building militant, class-conscious labour movements in certain periods, only to undermine the class independence of these movements through their popular front strategies in other periods.

Sections of the working class were able to make real material gains in exchange for hard and alienated labour for long periods of time in all three NAFTA countries. These gains underpinned the years of alienated prosperity for "privileged" sections of the working class. But that Faustian bargain is no longer possible as capitalists relentlessly push down wages, working conditions and living standards everywhere. Capitalists have constructed a

North American economic zone as well as a global one in which workers can more easily be played off against other workers. Solidarity in the context of regional and global downward harmonization has a fundamental dilemma: Who shall get the limited number of jobs? How will it be determined where business chooses to locate? Business freedom protected by pro-business governments and treaties that guarantee their rights give labour very little leverage. Workers and unions cannot challenge the power of business without solidarity, but solidarity is tremendously difficult to achieve in conditions of austerity and global downward harmonization. Solidarity can only be built on the bases of a struggle for upward harmonization, which would require regulating capital investment and labour markets, tasks that would require challenging the power of big business or struggling for a transformation of the economy from capitalism to one of socialist democracy, which would involve breaking the power of business. Either would require a powerful workers' movement, rooted in communities and workplaces, with a strategy of struggle and an alternative vision of society, a vision that rejects competition and embraces solidarity.

The present path of sectional, economistic and nationally-bound unionism using traditional collective bargaining methods is failing and is bound to fail in the neo-liberal global context. The current neo-liberal transformation of capitalism is reproducing many of the conditions that workers faced in the late-nineteenth and early twentieth century, but it is doing so in a globalized economy, not in a series of national economies. These very oppressive conditions could be the catalyst for the re-emergence of class-wide unionism aimed at transforming the system.

The Limits of Presently Existing Solidarity

Capitalists have created continental production chains and overlapping labour markets. Workers are objectively linked in these chains but the segmentation of organization, the economistic emphasis, the acceptance of competitive national capitalist strategies and the lack of consciousness of each other's struggles against the very same corporate strategies has limited continental responses of solidarity. Capitalism is a dynamic system, constantly transforming the composition of the working class, creating new cleavages as well as new bases of potential solidarity. Overcoming new and old cleavages and the fruition of these potentials for solidarity depends on the culture and politics of the labour movements. The intertwining of the continental production system and labour market means that working-class fightback has to transcend local and national boundaries lest business plays off workers in different regional and national locales. These new strategies and solidarities need to extend globally as well as continentally as migration patterns and production systems have themselves become more global. Marx's old slogan,

"Workers of the World, Unite," while faced with tremendous obstacles, has become more necessary and more possible than ever.

There is now an increasing basis and pressing need for greater continental labour solidarity, but the process towards a new continental labour movement will not be easy. The major corporations and the three governments will do whatever they can to prevent such a movement. The emergent culture and practice of solidarity, which will be discussed in Chapter 9, will assume many partial forms, some ad hoc, some more enduring. They will involve a variety of organizational forms and processes with varying geographical spread and degrees of intensity. The relatively more privileged working classes of the United States and Canada will have to be sensitive to the more extreme necessities of the Mexican working class for continental solidarity to have any possibility of success. They will have to accommodate their more exploited and oppressed Mexican brothers and sisters with a program that is neither protectionist or supportive of U.S. imperialism (Gindin 2004). The program will have to challenge the boundaries of neo-liberalism and the draining debt load suffered by Mexico. Projects and alliances will have to develop in ways that respect the national differences of the three working classes. This will require that the labour movements of the three North American countries develop a culture of international solidarity and a program that unites workers around their common interests rather than dividing them as competitors for scarce jobs. This new movement will have to create mechanisms to preclude domination by U.S. unions, which not only are numerically the largest but also are still in the process of overcoming their history as handmaidens of U.S. imperialism.

Workers are struggling — through the fog of old conceptions — to find more effective ways of fighting back. However, efforts at labour solidarity in the last decades, in general, have continued to reflect the fragmented and weak character of worker organization as well as its limited vision. This limited vision promoted accommodation — rather than challenges — to the boundaries of struggle set by the capitalist class, their governments and the new international treaties. No workers' movement can ignore the real constraints of bargaining and struggle, but they can be approached in different ways, as either accommodative or transformatory, to use Rebecca Johns's terms (1998). Johns has called "accommodative solidarity" the form of solidarity that supports struggles in foreign labour markets to protect jobs in the workers' home country even though humanitarian and solidaristic sentiments may also be involved. Accommodative solidarity has much in common with the economistic unionism that remains within a competitive, you-win-I-lose framework, which means that if some workers gain jobs, others lose them. The acceptance of these competitive boundaries promotes competition and the protection of some workers against other workers. Johns distinguishes this type of solidarity from what she calls "transformatory solidarity," a form of solidarity that seeks to transform the system that pits workers against each other. The latter challenges those limiting conditions that contribute to worker competition and enhance the power of capital. Protectionist solidarity is an expression of the character of fragmented, economistic unionism as well as of a notion of competitive working-class national interests.

Solidarity efforts have generally been confined to support for struggles in specific workplaces. Henry Frundt (2000) examined some of the solidarity efforts by U.S. unions in Mexico, Central America and the Caribbean and has classified them into four categories of cross-border organizing: international campaign organizing, clandestine targeting, federation-to-federation organizing and coalition organizing. International campaign organizing seeks to bring pressure on the parent company or contracting-out company. While international campaign organizing raises awareness in the home countries, promotes international networking on workers' rights and has had some victories, it does little to build unions that can endure when international attention fades. The second strategy, clandestine targeting, tries to organize a particular work place as a model with the hope of then expanding it to other workplaces. It is clandestine in that it builds the workers' network underground so the company can't fire the workers before they've achieved a certain level of strength. This mode of organizing has had some successes, but these successes rarely endure, as companies simply relocate or shift production to other plants. While the first two modes are mostly unidirectional, that is, with support coming from the north to the south, the third mode, federation-to-federation organizing, is the most bidirectional. An example of this is the alliance between the UE (United Electrical, Radio and Machine Workers of America) and the Frente Auténtico de Trabajo (FAT, Authentic Labour Front) that will be discussed in Chapter 9. The coalition organizing strategy uses a variety of models in its actual organizing practices. The distinguishing feature of coalition organizing is not its methods, but that it involves an alliance between different groups — church, labour and community. The limitation of all of these approaches is their focus on specific workplaces and their inability to address the general framework of capitalist power. Capital can freely close plants, relocate or switch contractors and generally has a state willing to repress labour rights in the interest of attracting capital. Even when these movements have strong aspects of social unionism — community involvement and coalitions around other forms of injustice — their potential is limited if they fail to act politically to address the framework that reproduces labour's subordination. The limited successes that have been achieved are not sustainable — and, in our view, cannot be sustainable — without a strong national labour movement and a political-juridical framework that is at least neutral, if not favourable, to workers' rights to collective organization.

Neither of these conditions exist in Mexico, and until they do, these efforts are doomed to ephemeral success, if any at all. This is not to say that these efforts have no value. They sow the seeds of cross-border solidarity, but the defeats can also be demobilizing and demoralizing.

Transforming Unionism, Transforming Solidarity, Transforming Society

Transformed unions could play a key role in building and sustaining a class-wide, transformatory workers' movement. Unions are the largest and most organizationally consolidated workers' organizations. Many unions have the resources to help sustain a plurality of smaller movements with weaker resource bases. Unions already have often played this crucial supportive role to weaker organizations and to broader coalitions for social justice. But they have often treated the challenge of building a class-wide movement as secondary to the more immediate concerns of their own union and its members, often committing only minimal resources and energy towards that long-term task. Collective bargaining law, bureaucratic caution and a sectoral, rather than a class-wide, focus have all contributed to a caution in protecting organizational survival and the short-term interests of their members. But the caution that sometimes served their interests in the past now threatens their members' interests and their organizational survival. The relentless neo-liberal offensive threatens the very existence of unions and the rights of collective bargaining. The labour movement must transform itself into a class-based, socio-political movement in order to challenge the existing framework of domination or it will continue to be crushed by it. Only an inclusive labour movement, centred on class-wide issues and fighting for social justice, will be capable of challenging the continuing attack on workers.

The transformation of unions must be internal as well as external. Unions must proactively fight racism and for women's rights. They need to promote leadership roles for women, visible minorities and immigrants through internal affirmative action programs to break down gender and racial divisions within the working class. Unions can be branches in the school of class struggle through which workers change themselves in the course of changing society. Unions can only play this role, however, if they are inclusive, participatory and democratic. They need internal processes through which workers develop their capacities as conscious activists and leaders. Only a movement with strong rank-and-file leaders has the potential to challenge the enormous power of business. The old IWW slogan "We are all leaders" has both a practical and ethical meaning. The development of rank-and-file leadership capacities is essential for the development of an effective and transformatory labour movement.

Working class solidarity, both national and international, requires a transformation of union organization and working class culture. Class-wide, feminist, anti-racist and internationalist concerns have to become real operating principles alongside more immediate and more sectoral concerns. International solidarity cannot be built on the basis of narrow, defensive and weak unionism. Solidarity today has to be international, inclusive and transformatory to be effective. It requires reinvigorated and transformed labour movements in all three NAFTA countries.

We will explore the embryonic beginnings of a continental labour movement in Chapter 9. But first, in Chapter 8, we'll examine the volatile situation of Mexico, a volatility that, whatever its outcome, will have a great impact on the possibilities for North America.

Chapter 8

Fighting Back
The Mexican Spark?

The continental integration promoted by NAFTA and corporate strategies brought together an explosive "Third World" country with two relatively stable capitalist democracies. All three countries have advanced capitalist production and a working class majority. Workers, in fact, often face the same corporations that use variants of the same strategies. But the situation, characteristics and context of the Mexican working class is radically different than that of their northern counterparts. The degree of exploitation and repression is much deeper, more widespread and much more severe. The working class still has strong revolutionary traditions radiating from a long history of popular uprisings and, most importantly, from the Mexican Revolution of 1910–20, an armed popular revolution that continues to be celebrated in popular culture and official events. And the regime context is one of great instability — a brutal drug war, increasing militarization and repression both in cities and the countryside and a regime with little legitimacy. The 2012 presidential election, which is widely seen in Mexico as having been manipulated by powerful big business forces (Roman and Velasco 2012a), on top of the presidential election frauds of 2006 and 1988 (Roman and Velasco 2012b), have deepened the skepticism of an electoral road to change. Mexico is heading towards a major implosion or explosion while continuing its increasingly deep integration into North America. Mexico's general volatility, including the overt counter-revolutionary processes and the more subterranean revolutionary processes that are taking place makes Mexico the weak link in the stability of capitalist North America. The implosion or explosion of Mexico will have dramatic ramifications for North America.

There is virtually no prospect of regaining and extending workers' rights in the framework of the present regime. In fact, the labour rights that are enshrined in the Mexican Constitution of 1917 and in later labour legislation are being further destroyed by the November 2012 reform of the LFT (Ley Federal del Trabajo). Article 123, the labour code of the Constitution, and subsequent implementing legislation represented a great victory for workers' rights, even though it also gave the government great powers for shaping the character of unionism. The degree to which these basic workers' rights were enforced varied from period to period and depended very much on the relative influence of different forces within the regime and the strength of particular unions. Labour law did give workers significant job security: employers had to justify layoffs and dismissals by showing that they faced special circumstances. Management authority was considerably restricted by labour law, and workers were aware that there were legal procedures through which they could challenge arbitrary managerial actions (Bortz 2008: 187–205). The LFT was long viewed by Mexican big business as an obstacle to their power and profits, but, in spite of the many successes of the big business offensive, they had long been blocked in achieving fundamental changes in the law. Popular opposition created hesitation in sections of the old ruling party, which along with the opposition of the electoral Left, stalemated the labour law reform. A radical de facto transformation of labour relations was well underway in the *maquila* regions and elsewhere in Mexico, but it lacked a legal underpinning and thus could be challenged. These changes in labour law have given extreme arbitrary power to business while maintaining the state's ability to prop up the official union oligarchy.

The changes to the LFT target both individual and collective rights of workers while preserving intact the mechanisms of undemocratic control by *charros*. The changes legalize outsourcing, allow for hourly rates of pay, make laying off and firing workers much easier by both increasing just grounds for them and sharply reducing severance pay obligations, limit back pay for unjust dismissals to one year, expand probationary and training contracts, undermine job security rights and increase managerial power by allowing for (more) use of unilateral measurements of productivity and worker performance. Under the old law, job security could be gained relatively quickly, workers had to be hired by the day, not the hour, and the workday was limited to eight hours; minimum wages were set by a tripartite committee of labour, business, and the government. These changes give the neo-liberal offensive against workers' rights a juridical underpinning and deepen its content. At the same time that workers' rights were being destroyed, the attempt to introduce democratic rights for union members was defeated. The proposal for secret ballot elections of union officials and the right for union members to see and ratify a new contract, though passed in the Senate, was removed in the lower house of Congress. Union officials in *charro* unions will continue to view how members vote and use violence, intimidation and other sanctions to control union elections. As well, collective bargaining contracts will continue to be negotiated secretly without members knowing what is in the contract until after it is signed.

Basic democratic and worker rights (freedom of association, the right to collective bargaining, the enforcement of labour standards, et cetera), many of which have been long violated in practice, are now being destroyed in law. The struggle for those rights would, sooner or later, have to spread to questions about the very nature of the Mexican regime and the continental integration process itself. These struggles, as well as Mexico's general volatility, would have major spillover effects in the rest of North America, given the trans-border character of the Mexican working class and the integrated character of much North American production. Major insurgency by the Mexican working class has the potential to be the spark of a North American labour insurgency, both through the spillover effects and through the example of struggle.

The weight of the Mexican working class within Mexico, its significant presence within the U.S. working class, its simultaneous national and transnational character, its revolutionary traditions and its dire and worsening situation create both a potential for a workers' insurgency in Mexico and for that insurgency to spread to the United States. Highlighting this special potential of the Mexican working class is not meant to suggest either that it is inevitable or that it would necessarily start in Mexico. However, within North America, Mexico is a likely starting point for such a development, and it would unavoidably take on a very radical character given the structure of oppression and traditions of violent repression in Mexico. And, if it starts elsewhere, the transnational Mexican working class has the weight and location to act as an agent of its spread and deepening. An insurgency could also start outside the working class — for example, among students — but its potential will be limited if the working class does not join the insurgency. The profound power of the capitalist class cannot be challenged without the working class as a central actor.

The prospects and character of a major labour insurgency in Mexico will both condition and be conditioned by other factors that could thwart, defeat or warp a workers' insurgency. The whole terrain of struggle could change because of the continuing escalation of the drug war, a complex war involving drug cartels, their governmental and military allies and the governments of both Mexico and the U.S. The continuing escalation of state violence and the cartel war, along with Mexico's economic depression, could intensify regional and cross-border migration, sharpening the political polarization within the United States over immigration and the "border crisis."

The struggle for economic survival and workers' rights in Mexico is taking place in the context of neo-liberal authoritarianism, a system that combines corrupt and constrained electoral competition with growing militarization and repression, all in the context of a deepening barbaric war for drugs, a prolonged crisis of legitimacy and economic depression. In fact, as discussed in Chapter 3, Mexico's "democratic transition" was partly fuelled by the hegemonic aspirations of an increasingly cohesive bourgeoisie seeking to wrest power from a semi-autonomous state elite. The middle classes, working class and popular sectors struggled for a genuinely democratic transition, but the tremendous power of the big capitalists, along with the authoritarian state apparatus, has constrained and warped the hoped-for democratic transition. This fluidity of the political regime creates a very different situation than in the United States and Canada, where the political context is fundamentally stable in spite of sharply increasing inequality and, in the case of the United States, political polarization. Mexico, however, is already in a period of decaying state institutions and internal warfare, warfare that has unleashed unprecedented violence and terror in many of the *maquila* areas, the areas of continentally integrated production. The repression of electoral and popular dissidence that accompanied electoral liberalization and the capitalist offensive has now moved to a much deeper, wider and more brutal level under the cover of "the war against drugs."

Mexico is the only country whose very institutional framework could be fundamentally challenged in the short and medium run. Mexican institutions are already under challenge by the drug wars. As well, the government is engaged in an anticipatory counter-insurgency to repress expressions of popular discontent, discontent that could grow with the continuing deterioration of human rights and economic conditions. Some areas are already under de facto military control and this could grow into disguised or open military rule in response to escalations in the drug war or in popular insurgency. This fundamental volatility is very different from the situation in Canada and the United States, where popular discontent may produce a growing insurgency against neo-liberal capitalism, but where the power and hegemony of capitalist democracy remains strong. But, in Mexico, there are only deformed fragments of capitalist democracy contained within a brutally repressive framework. The corporate offensive has almost completely destroyed the long-nurtured hopes of Mexicans for rising standards of living along with social and democratic rights. The fragmentation and crisis of domination in Mexico has coincided with a thirty- to forty-year attack on living standards and on social and democratic rights. The 2007–8 economic crisis has been devastating to Mexicans on both sides of the border. And, as elsewhere, the capitalist class continues to make the working and popular classes pay for the crisis. These ongoing effects of neo-liberalism and the new economic crisis create a very volatile situation in Mexico.

The drug wars have given cover for an intensification of governmental repression against popular protest. It has become highly dangerous to be a journalist in Mexico, especially if you report on corruption and collusion between the government and cartels. Seventy-four reporters have been killed and twelve have been disappeared between 2000 and 2011 (*La Jornada* 2011). As well, the drug war and the reign of terror of the drug cartels and the armed forces take place mainly in the northern areas where most of the *maquilas* are located. This creates a very dangerous and chilling location for organizing workers and protests.

Neither big business and its governmental allies nor the drug cartels would welcome a genuinely democratic transition, a transition in which pent-up social demands would burst forth in ways that would challenge their interests and the neo-liberal agenda. Mexico has a strong capitalist class, a class that is integrated into continental and global capital. U.S., Spanish, Canadian and other foreign big business have a powerful presence in Mexico alongside Mexican big business. Big business, whether Mexican or foreign, is not willing to have its interests challenged or to pay the costs of the crisis. And foreign corporations are also backed up by their own states as well as various international financial institutions. Big business and the U.S. government would attempt to prevent or defeat any popular threats to the neo-liberal agenda, whether they came electorally or through popular uprisings. The counter-revolutionary power of big business and the three NAFTA governments as well as that of capitalist international institutions would be exerted fully to prevent such an outcome. But the continuing economic crises and repression will continue to fuel popular discontent.

Mexico, contrary to widely held images outside Mexico, is not a predominantly rural country. Mexico is an urban, predominantly working-class country: 73 million of a total population of 115 million people live in cities with over 100,000 people. Sixty-four percent of Mexicans live in cities, only a slightly lower percentage than that of the U.S. (68 percent) and Canada (70 percent). Most of the economically active population in Mexico is waged or salaried — 75 percent or 32 million of an economically active population of 43.8 million (INEGI 2008). The size and concentration of Mexico's working class means that, should it develop a militant class-wide movement, it would have tremendous political weight.

Almost all of the working class has experienced decades of deterioration of wages and working conditions, now made even more acute by the recent economic crisis. The big business offensive, the failed democratic transition and the continuing extension and intensification of poverty and inequality have largely destroyed hope for change through individual effort or gradual reforms within the system. And the working class of Mexico still has revolutionary, collectivist and class-conscious rhetoric and traditions in spite of the ceaseless neo-liberal cultural offensive. The repertoire of popular protest in Mexico continues to have insurrectionary and revolutionary images and options. All of these factors point to the very real possibility of a major surge of working class protest in Mexico's near future. They suggest a significant potential for workers to emerge as actors in their own right and as a leading element of broader movements. The events in Oaxaca in 2006 exemplify this potential, where a strike by the democratic state section of the teachers' union evolved into a broad popular uprising that controlled the state's capital city for five months (Roman and Velasco 2008). The Mexican working class has the potential to be the force to lead a radical, democratic transformation of Mexico.

But the working class, as discontented as it is, has only found its voice and organization of collective resistance at local or fragmented national levels. Its potential has been thwarted by state repression and Mexico's industrial relations system. This system gives the state great control over whether a union will be recognized and which unions will be allowed to be recognized. A key part of that system has been *charrismo*, Mexico's quasi-corporatist state-linked union institutions. Mexico has the lowest union density of the three NAFTA countries: the 4.1 million unionized workers in Mexico constitute only 8.5 percent of the entire workforce (International Labour Organization). The International Labour Organization (ILO) estimates union density at 14.4 percent, but that figure is based only on the formal sector of the economy (International Labour Organization). The figure would be much higher were we to include the informal sector.

Mexican unions — excluding the vast majority that are phantom unions that only exist on paper — are hybrid institutions that blend features of a state institution, a party machine and an authoritarian union. Their leaders were part of a state-linked elite whose career path often flowed from their role in authoritarian unions to important positions in the ruling party, the government, state enterprise and even the private sector. Their personal advancement depended on controlling their members. They were the "labour lieutenants" of Mexico's one-party, state-guided capitalism and continue to play that role for Mexico's neo-liberal capitalism. They were an integrated part of the state system of labour control in Mexico's seventy-plus years of one-party rule and continue to be integrated into Mexico's current, more complex, fluid, and fragile system of labour control. They are not simply an authoritarian labour bureaucracy that can be challenged in the same way that authoritarian labour bureaucracies can be challenged in Canada and the United States. In the past, a challenge to the *charros* in any important sector was seen as a challenge to the state. Now, it is seen as a challenge to the new regime of neo-liberal authoritarianism.

The development of electoral competition and the control of the presidency by the conservative PAN from 2000–12 changed their mode and degree of integration with the state, but not their role as privileged agents of control over the working class. At the federal level, they developed an alliance of convenience with the conservative presidents even when they remained formally connected to the old ruling party. The teachers' union played a significant role in fraudulent maneouvers to deliver the 2006 presidential election to the PAN candidate, Calderón (Raphael 2007 : 279–96; López Obrador 2007: 234), for which they were rewarded by control of key positions of the federal education department. At the same time, the *charros* continued to play a more integral role in those cities and states where the PRI maintained governmental power. And that more integral role is being renewed at the national level with the presidential victory of Enrique Peña Nieto in July 2012, a victory in which the powerful heads of three undemocratic unions, the SNTE, the oil workers' union and the union of the IMSS played a major role.

These unions have long "represented" the organized sections of the working class in a corrupt and undemocratic manner. They, at times, delivered some benefits for their constituencies while using their control over workers to deliver even more benefits for themselves and for the major beneficiaries of the regime's development strategy (La Botz 1992: 103; Bensusán and Middlebrook 2012: 46–50; Raphael 2007: 230–55; Cano and Aguirre 2008: 237–62). These unions controlled labour market access, disciplined the work force, extorted money from workers and capital and used their labour-control role (both workplace and political) as part of their base for negotiating their interests with management and for their influence within the power bloc. The power and privilege of the "labour" elite required their ongoing control of unions and their related institutions. The government facilitated this control. This labour bureaucracy played, and continues to play, an important role in controlling the working class, which is the key reason that they continued to receive regime support even after the old ruling party lost the presidency to the PAN. However, containment of the working class by the *charros* was not simply based on their levers of bureaucratic and state-linked power. They were able to deliver significant economic benefits for important sectors of the working class for a long period of time, especially during the period of ISI development. These benefits included both direct wages and indirect wages (government subsidized housing and medical benefits for key sectors of the working class). These benefits are now being destroyed by the neo-liberal austerity policies. Another specific control mechanism was jobs for relatives of union members. But jobs, especially in the public sector, are being reduced. The material basis for *charro* control is being undercut by the very neo-liberal policies that the *charros* are helping to implement. Their control over workers is important to the neo-liberal project during the transition to even lower wages, more job insecurity and the continuing attempt to destroy any real unions. As well, the new political-electoral pluralism, as contained and deformed as it is, somewhat opens up new spaces of worker political protest that are likely to ramify back into the workplace and the stultified internal life of *charro* unions. There was a fit in the past one-party authoritarian regime of both citizens and union members as dependent clients. Workers' struggles against electoral fraud and the protection of existing labour rights are likely to spill over to growing demands for democratic rights in their unions.

The vast majority of Mexican workers do not belong to unions. Most workers who do belong to unions are members of *charro* unions. The struggle for democratic control of existing unions and building the union movement are two parts of the same struggle. They can't succeed without challenging the repressive structure of the Mexican state. The intensity of this struggle will reverberate throughout North America.

The strategic challenges faced by the Mexican working class are enormous. They have to battle for their rights in war zones, drug cartel–controlled zone, in zones under a de facto state of siege by the armed forces and more broadly in a legal framework aimed to deny freedom of association and individual workers' rights. Many of the most violent and repressive areas are areas that form part of continentally integrated production chains and have large, non-unionized working class populations. The struggle for elementary labour rights has to challenge the general institutional framework of repression but also the war on drugs and the cartels themselves, as the communitarian police forces have done in the state of Guerrero and as the Zapatistas have done in Chiapas (Gasparello 2009). Only a combative, robust, mass and inventive workers' movement can carry out these daunting struggles. Trade unionism, in any form, stands little chance of survival without a transformation of Mexico itself. Only a radicalized and reborn workers' movement can provide the organized core of such a movement for fundamental change. Workers' rights can only be won in Mexico through a radical transformation of Mexico itself.

The struggle of the Mexican working class takes place simultaneously in two countries. The deep integration of the Mexican working class in U.S. industrial production and services has important implications for the development of working-class movements in both countries. There are now many Mexican working-class families that are simultaneously part of two working classes in contiguous nations (Heyman 1991). The Mexican working class is unique among the three working classes of North America in that it straddles the border of two countries. Even though there is still significant labour market segmentation based on ethnicity and national origins, there is now an increasing mingling of working people (cf. Hansen 1990).

The Mexican and, more broadly, the Latina/o working class stands at the intersection of casualized labour inside the United States and super-exploited labour outside the United States. In both countries, they are largely denied the right of free association, the right to collective representation through unions. In the United States, these democratic rights are denied to most workers but most thoroughly to immigrants (Compa 2000). Mexican workers have to struggle on both sides of the border for elementary democratic rights that are denied by the historical system of labour control in Mexico, state legislation, their precarious legal status in the United States and neoliberalism in both countries.

The struggles in each society are likely to have both direct and indirect effects on the struggles in the other. Mexican workers — or members of the same working-class family — may be, at the same or different times, engaged in labour conflicts on both sides of the border. They may share similar work-related concerns. Mexican workers in the United States not only have ongoing links with their old communities but they have the potential of being important sources for the transmission of ideas, moods, tactics, strategies and formal links between workers on both sides of the border. The "making of the Mexican working class" has a strong trans-national character (cf. Thompson 1966).

Mexican workers inside the United States are simultaneously linked through their own lives, their families, their collective organizations and their work experiences to the Mexican working class in Mexico as well as and to the U.S. working class. There are the beginnings of formal transnational organizations of Mexican workers as well as myriad formal and informal links between Mexican communities on both sides of the border. The immigrant labour force provides a two-way transmission belt of people, ideas, and strategies. The role and politics of the Mexican transnational working class will be shaped by events and processes on both sides of the border.

An important example of this potential can be seen in the three revolts of Mexican workers in 2006, two of which occured in Mexico and one in the United States. Although the struggles were different in the two national contexts, these workers' mobilizations provide a glimpse of the potential for simultaneous struggles of the Mexican working class in both countries, struggles with a potential for convergence and synergy.

Vast sections of the Mexican working class — on both sides of the border — were in motion in the spring and summer of 2006 in three different insurgencies: the immigrant rights movement in the United States (Pallares and Flores-González 2010; González 2009), the Oaxaca uprising and commune (Roman and Velasco 2007) and the anti–electoral fraud movement in Mexico (Roman and Velasco 2012b).

The immigrant rights movement was a mass movement of immigrant workers, Latino communities of the U.S. and unions protesting proposed congressional legislation to criminalize not only undocumented immigrants but also those who offered them help. While this proposed legislation was the spark, the movement had deeper roots in the historic victimization of the Latino community, both immigrant and non-immigrant. The support among immigrants for the movement extended much beyond the Latino community into the Asian immigrant community. Over 250 mass marches were held in the U.S. in the spring of 2006. And, on May 1, there were marches in many U.S. cities that are estimated to have brought out between 3.5 and 5 million people (Pallares and Flores-González 2010: xv). There were also solidarity actions in Mexico.

The Oaxaca rebellion of 2006 had massive support from almost all sectors of the population, but the core of the movement was working class. The rebellion began when the government of the state of Oaxaca brutally attacked the downtown encampment of the striking Oaxaca teachers. The community immediately responded to the attack on the teachers as people rushed downtown to defend them. The battles between the police and the community developed into a massive uprising of workers and poor people, many of them Indigenous, from the city of Oaxaca and the surrounding areas. The people forced the police and Governor to leave the city, the state capital, and ran the city for over five months through a popular assembly. The movement was finally crushed by military action. The Oaxaca commune showed the potential for popular insurrection with the working class at its centre. It also showed the impossibility of sustaining an insurrectionary movement in one city alone. The movement, revolutionary in form and activity, but reformist in its simple, central demand — the removal of the Governor of the state by the federal government — could only survive in that temporary political conjuncture of spring-summer 2006. But the process shows the possibility of the working class in alliance with popular sectors to challenge the government and to run a city (Roman and Velasco Arregui 2007).

The third movement, the anti–electoral fraud mobilizations of the summer and fall of 2006, had a similar grassroots working-class base as the other two movements, but differed from them in important ways. Though there was great grassroots participation— hundreds of thousands of people protested the fraud in unprecedented street mobilizations that lasted for weeks — the grassroots did not control the movement. The movement was carefully controlled from above by the leadership of the "defeated" candidate, Andrés López Obrador. This leadership wanted to use the threat of disruption by the mass movement to pressure the electoral monitoring agencies to examine the fraud with honesty. But they did not want to lose control of the movement in ways that would scare business and the U.S., such as a general strike or factory occupations, or see the movement take actions that would provide an excuse for brutal state repression. Obrador's leadership therefore both mobilized and constrained popular energies: democratic decision-making processes were not developed; actions would be proposed by the leadership at mass rallies and would be ratified by the crowd without any discussions or proposed alternatives. The mass mobilizations were contained within the bounds of plebiscitarianism and elite bargaining strategies of the electoral Left-Centre.

All three of these movements were movements of Mexican workers fighting for human dignity and basic democratic rights, though, of course, in the United States, there were many other immigrant groups involved. The working-class character of these revolts has been obscured by their particularities. The core of the Oaxaca rebellion was the Oaxaca state teachers' union. Many of the leaders of the immigrant rights movement were working class and, often, union activists. And many of the activists of the anti–electoral fraud movement were also working class and activists in independent unions, in democratic currents in unions, or in neighbourhood associations. But the leadership of the movement was not working class. There were myriad informal linkages between all three of these struggles, though they never converged into one movement. The political spectrum in each of the movements was not identical, the goals varied and the contexts were different. The fact that the Mexican working class was in motion on both sides of the border in a historically unprecedented way, however, indicates the potential for these movements to have a major impact on class struggle in North America.

The tremendous ferment of the Mexican working class on both sides of the border in 2006 has been dampened by defeats, demoralization and co-optation (González 2009). The conditions that produced these movements not only persist but, in the economic sphere (jobs, income, and poverty) they have sharply worsened since the 2008 crisis. These three movements have shown another face of continental workers' solidarity, the face of rank-and-file workers' struggles, struggles that were sometimes connected through informal networks among Mexico's trans-border working class.

These struggles were not mainly driven by narrow economic goals but by a demand for democratic rights and dignity by ordinary working people. All three of these struggles of Mexican workers were political, economic and social at the same time. None of the goals of these movements can be achieved by trade union struggle alone. The premise that has so poorly served unionism, that trade union struggles could proceed largely independent of political and social struggles, has been demolished, in practice, by globalization and the corporate political offensive against unions of the last thirty-five years. The formidable challenge for the Left is to find ways to foster convergence of these struggles without subordinating the particular needs and demands of each struggle.

The Mexican–U.S. transnational movements have the potential to inspire and energize the North American labour movement as the 1994 Zapatista uprising did for youth worldwide. As well, Mexican workers in the United States are living links between the Mexican, the Canadian and the U.S. working classes. They are concentrated in the increasingly non-union private sector. Many of those in unions — and many that could become members with an expansion of unionism in the United States — would be members of U.S.–Canadian binational unions. Their location inside the U.S. working class, their present or potential membership in U.S.–Canadian binational unions and their continuing formal and informal links to Mexico mean that they could play a key role in the forging of a new continental unionism in North America.

The role of the cross-border Mexican working class as well as the potential for cross-border class solidarity will be significantly influenced by developments in the organized labour movements of North America. A combative, class-inclusive and anti-racist response by Canadian and U.S. labour would dramatically increase the likelihood for solidarity and successful struggle in all three countries. The organized labour movement has the potential of contributing to the development of a new culture of solidarity in North America, a culture that builds on the transnational links and identities of Mexican workers and extends the boundaries of that solidarity to encompass the whole of the working class of North America.

The Mexican working class is rich in traditions of struggle and collectivity but weak in terms of organization and resources. The Canadian and U.S. labour movements, as weakened and under attack as they are, are rich in resources and organization. The struggle of Mexican workers for workers' rights and genuine unions takes place under an exceptionally dangerous and repressive situation. They need international solidarity from their richer and more organizationally consolidated sister organizations to the north. They need a solidarity of shared struggle that recognizes the combined national and international character of class struggle. Each movement needs autonomy to operate as it sees fit in its national space. Material aid has to come with no strings attached. There are the beginnings of this kind of solidarity, but these beginnings remain encased in continuing strategies of competitiveness. The reinvention of the labour movement will come from creative struggles from below, such as the immigrant rights' movement in the U.S., in synergy with changes in culture, perspective and organizational structure of unions themselves. New strategies of organizing and mobilizing are essential. Workers and unions in all of North America are under a common attack. They need to fight back with continental and class-wide transformatory solidarity.

Chapter 9

Fighting Back

The Seeds of Worker Continentalism

Both the Canadian Labour Congress (CLC) and the AFL-CIO (U.S.) supported trade liberalization from the 1920s to the mid 1970s (Robinson 2002; Kay 2001: 51; Smith 1992). Exports by U.S. companies had created more jobs for Americans and both exports and foreign investment were important job creators in Canada. But when free trade came to mean job losses rather than job gains, both labour movements reversed their earlier positions on trade. In the case of the U.S., when imports from Asia began to cost American jobs, some unions responded with protectionist positions that, at times, slid into racism and the scapegoating of foreign workers. Two examples of this response were the protectionist "Buy American" campaigns and the racist, anti-Japanese sentiments expressed around the auto industry. While protectionism is not necessarily racist, these campaigns sometimes became enmeshed with racism, as in the campaign against Japanese car imports (Kay 2011: 53). These America-first responses had little positive effect for workers. In fact, the job losses were only partly caused by imports. They were also linked to the big business offensive that included downsizing as well as relocation to non-union areas, both made more feasible by technological change. The initial fear of job losses focused on Asia, only turning to Mexico later. This focus on cheap foreign labour as the cause of job loss played into the divide-and-rule strategy of business. As well, it obscured the fact that it was U.S. companies themselves that were relocating directly or through subcontracting as well as carrying out the assault on workers' rights in the U.S. This focus sidetracked workers from the difficult task of organizing more workers and carrying out an effective fightback against big business. The loss of manufacturing jobs to overseas production combined with government and corporate attacks have led to a tremendous loss of union membership in the last few decades.

The CLC's shift away from a free trade approach has important parallels with that of the AFL-CIO. But the major role of foreign, especially U.S., capital in the Canadian economy, led to important differences. Canada was not the leading imperial power but a country in which the top layers of capital were composed of both U.S. and Canadian capitalists. Canadian labour's turn away from free trade led it to an economic nationalism that was importantly different from the economic nationalism of labour in the world's leading imperial power. U.S. labour, at that time, did not fear foreign domination of their economy. They saw foreign workers, not foreign ownership, as the source of their problems. Canadian labour, however, saw both as a source of their problems.

The Canadian economy was both growing and becoming more integrated into the U.S. economy in the 1960s. The CLC, in this period, did not oppose the high level of foreign investment in the Canadian economy, though it expressed sympathy for proposals to regulate it made by others (Smith 1992: 41–42). The CLC supported free trade through the GATT (General Agreement of Tariffs and Trade) in the 1960s and early 1970s, even while recognizing that some industries would be hurt by tariff reductions. William Dodge, the Secretary-Treasurer of the CLC, responded to criticism of the free trade position of the CLC: "'As a Congress we have to think of the interests of the economy as a whole and the effects of restrictive trade approaches in the economy as a whole'" (quoted in Smith 1992: 43). And, in response to challenges from the Left nationalist Waffle, the Research Director of the CLC "argued that Canada would not have been able to develop without U.S. capital," and "that breaking with the U.S. would be 'committing economic suicide'" (Smith 1992: 43). This continentalist position would begin to shift with the government's imposition of wage controls in 1975. The CLC was forced to reconsider its position and moved towards the economic position that it had rejected so strongly previously:

> By 1988, the CLC viewed continental integration and U.S. multinational presence in Canada not as the indispensable conditions for Canadian economic development and employment, but as obstacles to these goals. Furthermore, continental integration was viewed as a Trojan horse that would allow the Tories to consolidate their roll-back of the state, evident in a variety of initiatives ranging from privatization of state-run concerns to cuts in social spending. (Smith 1992: 54)

But, as Smith argues, the economic nationalism of the CLC was one that included proposals for tripartite consultations and policies promoting Canadian capitalist development. The CLC remained firmly embedded in the notion of working with your own capitalists to become more competitive and keep jobs in your country, as did the AFL-CIO. This strategic entrapment within the boundaries of capitalism has led to policies of concessions and joint union-company campaigns for government subsidies. The preservation of jobs through concessions and state subsidies may lead to a reprieve of job losses for a period, but, in the longer run, it contributes to the downward harmonization of wages and working conditions and the upward harmonization of hand-outs to companies, hand-outs paid for by the working class through taxation. As well, big business and neo-liberal governments had little interest in labour as an ally in national capitalist development. The regional and global stage was a superb setting for intensifying their divide-and-rule strategy.

The tremendous defeats suffered by workers and unions in Canada and the U.S., along with the new realities of CUFTA, NAFTA and capitalist globalization, led workers to search for new answers. A new internationalism and, more specifically in North America, a new trinationalism, has begun to emerge, but these hopeful beginnings, which will be discussed below, remain embedded in the old notions and practices of competitiveness. This tension in trade unionism between sectional unionism and a transformatory, class-wide movement continues to be a central problem for the labour movement and cannot be overcome within a competitive framework. The resolution of this tension requires moving beyond competition towards a strategy and program for solidarity, one that will unavoidably need to challenge the power of big business.

The proposal for a North American free trade agreement had elicited a strong negative response from the Canadian and U.S. trade union movement. They saw this agreement as another part of the big business offensive against workers. The Canadian labour movement had recently engaged in a massive mobilization in alliance with many other groups that failed to stop the Canada–U.S. free trade agreement. U.S. unions, on the other hand, had not been very concerned with CUFTA as they didn't perceive it as a threat. But both Canadian and U.S. labour would later see the proposed NAFTA as a big threat.

However, in Mexico, the *charro* leaders gave full support to NAFTA, while the AFL–CIO and the Canadian Labour Congress (CLC) argued that NAFTA was an attack on workers in all three countries. The *charros*, members of the state-party elite, saw the prospect of jobs moving to Mexico as an opportunity to expand their dues-paying base and to sell more protection contracts. Furthermore, the promise of new jobs for a desperate workforce gave NAFTA some appeal among workers in Mexico. While the AFL–CIO and CLC asserted that NAFTA was an attack on workers in all three countries, the *charros*, without any interest in solidarity, argued that this was simply protectionism on the part of more privileged workers. This argument, although used opportunistically, had considerable credibility, given that many U.S. and Canadian unions have a long history of protectionism and competitive alliances with corporations and various levels of government and endeavour to attract business away from other locations — and other workers.

This argument, however, fails to recognize the alternative and emergent currents and tendencies in U.S. and Canadian unionism, tendencies being strengthened by the necessity of finding adequate responses to continentalism, globalization and the changing composition of the labour force through immigration from the Third World. Instead of seeking to build transformatory solidarity instead of protectionism and protectionist solidarity, the *charros* sought to close all doors to solidarity in their own interests and the interests of big business.

The Congreso del Trabajo (Labour Congress) gave unqualified support to their government's proposals for NAFTA, a NAFTA without any protection for workers, whereas U.S. and Canadian unionists lobbied against the adoption of NAFTA. The main union federations in Mexico were totally unsympathetic to proposals by U.S. and Canadian labour for enforceable labour provisions. This stance of Mexico's official unions meant that U.S. and Canadian unions would have to seek out other Mexican partners in the fight against NAFTA.

A variety of organizations from Canada and Mexico — labour, farmer, consumer, human rights and environmental — met in October 1990 to discuss plans for opposing free trade in North America. U.S. and Canadian organizations then met the following month. While the CLC and the AFL-CIO were deeply involved, Mexico's main labor federation, the Confederación de Trabajadores de México (CTM, Confederation of Mexican Workers), was not. The CTM strongly supported the free trade proposal, as did the independent STRM (Sindicato de Telefonistas de la República de Mexican, Union of Telephone Workers of the Mexican Republic). The search for Mexican labour allies, given the support of free trade by the officialist unions, led Canadian and U.S. labour to work with the Frente Auténtico de Trabajo (FAT, Authentic Labour Front), a small, independent federation strongly opposed to neo-liberalism and free trade. The FAT is a small federation composed of union, farmer, community and neighbourhood associations that is internally democratic and independent of Mexico's official unions. Previously, the links between Canadian, U.S. and Mexican labour had either been episodic and at the local level or between the northern federations and Mexico's official federation. This new trinational labour alliance fought together against the creation of NAFTA and, when its passage seemed inevitable, they fought for the inclusion of effective labour and environment clauses. These contacts and shared struggles led to the formation of deeper links between specific unions.

The fight against NAFTA had brought together labour and other groups from the three countries, though they failed both in their efforts to stop NAFTA and to get enforceable labour and environment standards included in the treaty itself. The Clinton Administration, as a token concession to labour and environmental groups, added toothless side agreements on each of these issues. Unlike trade and investment, however, labour and the environment did not receive protection under NAFTA. Both side agreements were symbolic and had no serious enforcement mechanism. The failure to achieve enforceable accords was seen as a big defeat for labour and environmental groups.

Norman Caulfield has argued that the failure to create a supranational law and the continued supremacy of domestic labor law provided an incentive for downward harmonization:

> The domestic supremacy of labor law and especially how it is enforced preserves an incentive for businesses to invest in the territory with the least effective level of worker protection. This leaves the NAALC [North American Agreement on Labor Cooperation] signatories with incentive to attract investment through the deregulation of their respective labor law regimes. The reformed Mexican labour law to allow more flexibility for business to determine wages and conditions is indicative of this development. The ironic result is that, instead of strengthening labor standards, the NAALC, has contributed to their weakening. More specifically, the NAALC has been completely inadequate in correcting the verified record of nonenforcement of labor laws in Mexico, particularly with regard to freedom of association, the foundation upon which all other workers' rights rest. (Caulfield 2010: 68)

The specific criteria of adherence or violation of the NAALC's eleven, very general labour rights principles is based on whether the government of each country is enforcing its own labour laws. The procedures for handling complaints vary depending on the type of labour issue but, in terms of remedies, they are useless (Kay 2001: 114; Faux 2006: 143). The Commission for Labor Cooperation is composed of a Secretariat and a Ministerial Council, the latter being made up of the Secretary of Labor of both the U.S. and Mexico, and of the Minister of Labour of Canada. Each country has a National Administrative Office (NAO) to which complaints can be filed. Complaints sent to the NAO can be sent to the Ministerial Council for consultations. If unresolved at that level, depending on their character, an Evaluation Committee of Experts (ECE) can be convened to investigate the complaint, and, finally, an arbitral panel can be convened. Only an arbitral panel can impose sanctions, and this can only occur if the issue is related to trade and is "covered by mutually recognized labor laws" (Kay: 114). No complaints have ever been sent to an ECE or an arbitral panel in the fifteen years from 1994–2008 (Kay: 115). Kay outlines the NAALC's weaknesses:

> The NAALC unequivocally has weak enforcement mechanisms, and therefore weak redress effects. It grants some labor rights less protection than others, prohibits all types of violations from reaching the highest level in the adjudicatory hierarchy, and provides insufficient penalties. Every labor activist I interviewed agreed that NAALC is

woefully inadequate as a tool for redressing labor rights violations across the continent. (Kay 2011: 163)

The title of a section of Jeff Faux's book describes the uselessness of NAALC vividly: "NAFTA's Penalty for Mistreating Workers: Nothing" (2006: 142). The procedures for evaluating violations make sure that no enforcement takes place. As Faux has said, if a government violates its labor laws, nothing happens:

> The ultimate penalty for Group 1 violations is that the labor ministers meet and talk. That's it. The penalty for Group 2 violations is that ministers talk and a committee of experts evaluate. That's it. On paper, the ultimate penalty for Group 3 violations is a fine or sanction. (Faux 2006: 143)

But the latter has never happened.

Recent developments between unions in the U.S., Mexico and Canada, as preliminary as they are, provide a glimmer of hope or, at least, an indication of a direction for the future. Most of the initial contacts between unions and union federations from the three countries were initially in relation to fighting the NAFTA proposal, then fighting for enforceable labour provisions, then attempting to use the labour side accord to protect workers' rights. Kay argues that the specific institutional arrangements of NAALC unintentionally fostered transnational solidarity. The provision that a complaint against a government had to be filed "outside the country in which a violation occurred" meant that workers and unions in one country needed support from workers and unions in another country (Kay 2011: 118). This provision fostered the joint filing of many of the complaints by unions and other organizations from more than one country. This was in sharp contrast to complaints to the equivalent environmental commission, for which complaints were filed only with one agency. Most of the labour complaints were filed jointly by organizations from two or three countries, whereas almost all of the environmental complaints were filed by organizations from only one country (Kay 2011: 24).

It was the common opposition to NAFTA that brought together the leadership of the UE (United Electrical, Radio and Machine Workers of America) with that of the FAT at the October 1991 conference against continental free trade in Zacatecas, Mexico; the two unions had not had any previous relationship. Both FAT and the UE are small organizations on the margins of the main labour movements but both have histories of militancy. The UE has lost many members as electronics plants moved to the *maquila* regions of Mexico.

The UE and FAT formed a "Strategic Organizing Alliance" in 1992 with the purpose of building "a new kind of international solidarity focused on organizing and based on rank-and-file involvement" (United Electrical Radio and Machine Workers of America, n.d). The principles of this alliance are outlined on their website:

> First, [the Strategic Organizing Alliance] is a relationship based on mutual respect — on solidarity, not charity. Second: it is based on communication with clarity about decision-making: the FAT is responsible for final decisions regarding work in Mexico, as the UE is for work in the U.S. Third: we have tried to do things in a bilateral way: so with worker to worker exchanges, UE members have travelled to Mexico and members of the FAT have come to the U.S. (United Electrical Radio and Machine Workers of America, n.d)

As Kay points out, both organizations sought to build a long-term relationship rather than episodic solidarity:

> Rather than run to the border for support at a moment of crisis, the UE and FAT decided to build a relationship that could provide ongoing support. FAT and UE leaders imagined that together they could potentially even avert crises by working toward upward harmonization of wages and working conditions in North America and by undermining the ability of companies to pit them against each other. (Kay 2011: 173)

The relationship between the FAT and the UE is based on principles of horizontal solidarity in spite of significant differences in resources and in their national political contexts. FAT and UE have also played an important role in the development of broader coalitions of unions across the continent. But their organizing efforts in Mexico have had very little success in spite of important efforts at international solidarity (Kay 2011: 173–74; Hathaway 2000: 176–80). The failure to win durable victories, let alone to make a breakthrough in organizing, is partly related to the weakness of the FAT. But this failure is also related to the power of the companies and the Mexican government to prevent independent unions from surviving. The challenge of making an organizing breakthrough is enormous and would necessitate much greater resources as well as a strategy for challenging Mexico's straight-jacket of labour repression, a straight-jacket that has been significantly tightened by the recent changes in Mexican labour law, a topic that will be discussed later in this chapter.

The USW (United Steel Workers, 850,000 members) and the Mineros (SNTMMSRM/Los Mineros, 180,000 members[1]) have taken the first steps towards forming a continental union. This is the most significant union initiative at a continental level since the start of NAFTA in 1994. The relationship began with solidarity actions by miners in Mexico during a 2005 strike in Arizona against the mining giant ASARCO/Grupo Mexico, which led, later that year, to the signing of a solidarity pact between the two unions. When the miners in Cananea, Sonora, Mexico, started their protracted and bitter strike in 2007 against the same company, the Arizona miners and the USW gave them support. In both cases, workers crossed the border for solidarity picketing. As well, the USW's Women of Steel started to raise funds for the families of the striking Cananea miners. There had been an explosion at another Grupo Mexico mine in Pasta de Conchos, Coahuila in 2006 in which sixty-five miners were killed. The government and the company started an intensive campaign to destroy the union and imprison its leader, Napoleón Gómez Urrutia, after he accused them of "industrial homicide" over the Pasta de Conchos disaster. They charged Gómez Urrutia with acts of corruption, charges from which he has since been cleared by the Mexican courts (La Botz 2010b). Gómez Urrutia took refuge in Vancouver, Canada, in 2006 with the support of the USW and works from the USW District 3 office in Burnaby, B.C. Gómez Urrutia has continued to lead his union from exile: the Mineros have continued militant struggles and have won victories in spite of brutal repression. In 2010, the two unions agreed to form a cross-border commission to explore unification, and in 2011 they elaborated the transitional processes that would involve more integration while remaining, for the time being, separate unions (McKay 2011; LaBotz 2010a; also United Steelworkers, n.d.)

The USW is also involved in an attempt to form a global union with UNITE, a major union from Great Britain and Ireland:

> Workers Uniting is the name of the new international union created by Unite — the biggest union in the U.K. and the Republic of Ireland and the USW — the biggest private sector union in the U.S. and Canada. (United Steelworkers, n.d.)

The Mineros, presumably, would also be part of this global union if the merger between the Mineros and USW goes forward.

Ken Neumann, the USW Canadian National Director, reviewed the history of this relationship with the Mineros when he addressed the 2012 convention of Los Mineros in Mexico City on May 3, 2012:

> When we began this fight in solidarity with Los Mineros more than six years ago, we did not know how hard it would be or how much it would cost. We knew only that the members of Los Mineros and the United Steelworkers work in the same industries and for the same companies ... We knew only that if we did not stand with workers in Mexico to fight for higher wages and better living conditions, then

our own wages in Canada and the United States would be driven downward. We knew only that when our members were on strike at Grupo Mexico in 2005, Los Mineros walked our picket lines and stopped work in solidarity.

We knew only that here was a union — Los Mineros — and a leader — Napoleón Gómez — who believed that Mexican workers had the right to good wages and benefits and dignity and respect, who were willing to fight for this right, and who understood that it was necessary and possible to build a single union representing mine, metal, steel and manufacturing workers from the southern border of Mexico to the Arctic Circle. (United Steelworkers, 2012)

The idea of a common union, still an aspiration rather than a reality, is a more organic commitment to solidarity than previous attempts at cross-border co-operation. The development of a common union or, at least, more formalized organizational connections creates a framework in which cross-border worker interaction and solidarity could grow. A common union would also require some kind of federative character that accorded each national labour component a large degree of autonomy in order to avoid domination by the larger or wealthier national sectors and to allow for flexibility in dealing with national and sub-national governments.

The dilemmas of a trinational union would be even more difficult than those already present in existing national or transnational unions. Uneven development and potential competition within the union is an issue faced by all national and transnational unions. These dilemmas would be tougher given the much greater gap between Mexico and its northern neighbours in labour standards and incomes, but a common union would create a framework in which the workers themselves could sort through the issues of solidarity and try to avoid the divide-and-rule strategy of business. There are no guarantees of success and there are serious dangers to the formation of a continental union. But these dangers pale in comparison to those of a North American labour movement that remains as divided and competitive as at present, and the awareness of these dangers could help workers and union members avoid them.

Most of labour's efforts to develop continental solidarity have taken place among private sector unions or federations (UE/FAT, USW/Mineros). But NAFTA specifically and the corporate offensive more generally have also targeted the public sector for downsizing, cutting costs, privatization, and promoting more positive views towards business (Emery and Ohanian 2004). NAFTA directly promotes the privatization of education through Chapter 11, the section protecting investors' rights, which establishes education as an area of investment and calls for equal treatment of foreign investors (Luz Arriaga

1999: 145). While the core struggles of teachers have been within their localities and nations, they have also responded continentally by organizing the Trinational Coalition to Defend Public Education. The Trinational Coalition does not have formal membership but has strong, active participation by many teachers' federations in Canada and the two-hundred-thousand-strong dissident teachers' current within the national *charro* teachers' union in Mexico. The Coalition does not have a permanent organization and receives all of its funding from unions.

In Canada, the Canadian Teachers' Federation has played a key role from the start by promoting the Coalition in provincial organizations and by co-ordinating solidarity actions. Several provincial organizations have also been very active in the coalition: the British Columbia Teachers Federation, the Ontario Secondary School Teachers Federation, the Manitoba Teachers Society and the Fédération nationale des enseignantes et des enseignants du Québec and the Confédération des syndicats du Québec. More recently, the Canadian Association of University Teachers joined in the work of the coalition, including being host of the sixth conference in Toronto in May 2003 (Leahy 2010).

The Mexican participants in the Coalition include the CNTE, the dissident teachers' organization that has existed within the national *charro* teachers' union since 1970. As well, several university unions also participate. The National Education Association in the U.S. and the American Federation of Teachers, while expressing sympathy for the project, have not been very involved. Beyond sharing experiences and discussing how to fight back against the corporate assault, the Canadian participants have mobilized letter-writing and other support campaigns for the Mexican teachers who face constant and often violent repression. While these links are relatively minimal, they are important. They provide an arena in which experiences can be shared and strategies discussed, a process from which stronger sentiments and strategies of solidarity can emerge (Luz Arriaga 1999; Leahy 2010).

Though there is a growing awareness that the fightback needs to be continental, if not global, the implications of the two long-existing transnational workers' relationships in North America have not been strategically grasped. These two sets of binational working-class relations could provide the core elements for the building of a continental labour movement, one that could create new and more effective forms of national and trinational struggle.

The 2006 movements, the organizational explorations between the USW and the Mineros, the strategic organizing alliance between the UE and FAT, the Trinational Coalition for the Defence of Public Education, the formation of the Tri-National Solidarity Alliance are expressions of labour solidarity that have given us a glimpse of the potential for the emergence of a new continental workers' movement. These emergent forms of continental class solidarity will be diverse and their specific contours are hard to foresee. But the intensity of economic relations between the industries of these countries along with the binational character of the Mexican working class and the binational character of U.S.–Canadian unions creates great potential. The development of that potential will hinge, on two crucial and inter-related processes: 1) the further development of ideological, strategic and organizational links among these movements and, crucially, for the case of the United States, the development of similar links between the Mexican immigrant workers in the United States and the rest of the American working class (non-immigrant Mexican and Latina/o workers, other immigrant workers, white and Black "American" workers); and 2) the transformation of unions and union cultures so that they become the vehicles and expression of these linkages among workers. Our emphasis on the specially located Mexican working class does not mean we are dismissive of the important role and potential of Black, white, Latino and immigrant workers in the United States, but we are emphasizing a unique complex of characteristics that gives the Mexican working class a special potential. Some of these characteristics are shared by other segments of the immigrant and non-immigrant working class. As well, these other segments may have other characteristics that could promote and energize protest movements. The spark and the fuel can come from different sources.

It is not possible to predict where the spark for a spread of insurgencies will begin: the unexpected uprising in Tunisia inspired the Arab Spring, and the Occupy Wall Street movement in New York inspired similar movements all over the world. These exemplary insurgencies help overcome the fatalistic acceptance of injustice and oppression. The capitalists have provided an abundance of kindling in the United States, Canada and Mexico alike. But the explosive character of the Mexican situation combined with the weight and militant traditions of the Mexican working class gives it great potential for providing the spark. Furthermore, the deeply rooted presence of Mexican workers on both sides of the U.S. border would make a spread of a workers' insurgency to the United States all the more likely.

The seeds of a new workers movement have been planted. Their growth depends on the conscious efforts by workers and unions at a multitude of sites and levels of struggle as well as alliances with other social sectors — students, small farmers and intellectuals. The old worlds of capitalism have been built on the backs of successive generations of workers. A new world of equality and justice can be built by workers and ordinary people themselves. But this will only be possible with the creation of a new workers' movement, a movement where "Solidarity Everywhere" is merged with "Solidarity Forever" and moves from the realm of rhetoric and the margins of practice to the centre of workers' culture and practice.

132

The crucible of North American transformation is heating up, but its outcome is far from clear. There is a growing clash between the continuing corporate neo-liberal offensive and the embryonic forces of resistance. The same powerful forces that unleashed the neo-liberal transformation of North America are now using the economic crisis as their new rationale for continuing their offensive. The deepening attack on public sector unions in all three NAFTA countries as well as the ongoing cuts to social spending reflect the continuation of the offensive started by big business forty years ago. The Occupy Wall Street protests, the mobilizations of public sector unions in Wisconsin and Ohio, the student protest movement in Quebec on tuition increases and the 2012 student movement in Mexico against electoral fraud and media monopoly reflect the discontent engendered by this offensive (Roman and Velasco 2012a). Income polarization, growing poverty, insecure employment, loss of pensions and benefits and the attack on social services were all way underway before the crisis. The combination of the ongoing economic crisis, the continuing polarization of income and wealth, the growing clashes over public sector cuts and union rights and the global Occupy movements all point to the likelihood of an exceptionally volatile period for North America. This volatility is likely to sharply increase — especially in Mexico, given the multiple crises occurring there. The combination of the continuing — and possibly deepening — economic recession and the very polarized politics of Mexico and the United States will make the coming period in those countries turbulent.

The alchemists of the corporate offensive have thrown social rights, decent jobs and public well-being into the continental crucible in the hope that it will produce shiny gold to line their pockets. But the intense heat in the crucible may produce a different outcome. Rather than gold to line the pockets of the corporate alchemists, the intense heat may produce the energetic and resolute re-emergence of the salt of the earth, the working classes of the continent, imbued with a renewed determination to build a new North America.

Note
1. Sindicato Nacional de Trabajadores Mineros, Metalúrgicos, Siderúrgicos y Similares de la República Mexicana, National Union of Mine and Metal Workers of the Mexican Republic, Los Mineros, Mexican Miners Union.

References

Albo, Gregory. 2002. "Neoliberalism, the State, and the Left: A Canadian Perspective." *Monthly Review* 54, 1 (May).

Andreas, Peter. 1998. "The U.S. Immigration Control Offensive: Constructing an Image of Order on the Southwest Border." In Marcelo M. Suárez-Orozco (ed.), *Crossings: Mexican Immigration in Interdisciplinary Perspectives*, 343–356. Cambridge: Harvard University Press.

Arriaga Lemus, Maria de la Luz. 1999. "NAFTA and the Trinational Coalition to Defend Public Education." *Social Justice* 26, 3 (Fall)

Banco de México. 2012. *Informe Anual 2011 — Cuadro Remesas desde el exterior a la economía mexicana*. México: Banxico.

Barton, Josef. 2004. "Borderland Discontents: Mexican Migration in Regional Contexts, 1880–1930." In Marc C. Rodriguez (ed.), *Repositioning North American Migration History*. Rochester: University of Rochester Press.

Bensusán, Graciela, and Kevin J. Middlebrook. 2012. *Organized Labour and Politics in Mexico: Changes, Continuities and Contradictions*. London: Institute for the Study of the Americas, University of London.

Bortz, Jeffrey. 2008. *Revolution within the Revolution: Cotton Textile Workers and the Mexican Labor Regime 1910–1923*. Stanford: Stanford University Press.

Bradford Neil. 1998. *Commissioning Ideas: Canadian National Policy Innovation in Comparative Perspective*. Toronto: Oxford University Press Canada.

Brecht, Bertolt. 1935. "Questions From a Worker Who Reads." At <marxists.org/subject/art/literature/brecht/index.htm>.

Bronfenbrenner, Kate. 1997. "The Effect of NAFTA on Union Organizing." *New Labour Forum* 1 (Fall): 50–60.

Bureau of Labor Statistics, U.S. Department of Labor. n.d.a. Based on the series "Unemployment Rate — Hispanic or Latino." Washington, DC. At <http://www.bls.gov/data/>.

___. n.d.b. Based on the series "Employment — Part-time workers Hispanic or Latino." Washington, DC. At <http://www.bls.gov/data/>.

___. n.d.c. Based on the series: "Unemployment Rate — 16 to 24 years, Black or African American." Washington, DC. At <http://www.bls.gov/data/>.

Business Council on National Issues. 2001. "Reflections on a Quarter Century of Business Leadership on Behalf of Enterprise and Country: A Conversation with Thomas d'Aquino President and Chief Executive on the Occasion of the 25th Anniversary of the Business Council on National Issues." May 9. At <ceocouncil.ca/wp-content/uploads/archives/speeches_2001_05_09.pdf>.

Camfield, David. 2011. *Canadian Labour in Crisis: Reinventing the Workers' Movement*. Black Point, NS: Fernwood.

References

Canadian Council of Chief Executives. n.d. "About CCCE." At <ceocouncil.ca/about-ccce>.

Cano, Arturo, and Alberto Aguirre. 2008. *Doña Perpetua: El poder y la opulencia de Elba Esther Gordillo*. Mexico: Grijalbo.

Carroll, William K. 2004. *Corporate Power in a Globalizing World: A Study in Elite Social Organization*. Toronto: Oxford University Press.

Carroll, William K., and Murray Shaw. 2001. "Consolidating a Neoliberal Policy Bloc in Canada, 1976–1996. *Canadian Public Policy* XXVII, 2.

Caulfield, Norman. 2010. *NAFTA and Labor in North America*. Urbana: University of Illinois Press.

CEPAL/ECLAC (Comisión Económica para América Latina y el Caribe/Economic Commission for Latin America and the Caribbean). 2011. *Panorama Social de América Latina*. Santiago, Chile: CEPAL/ECLAC.

Clarkson, Stephen. 2002. *Uncle Sam and Us: Globalization, Neoconservatism, and the Canadian State*. Toronto: University of Toronto Press.

Cohen, Deborah. 2011. *Braceros: Migrant Citizens and Transnational Subjects in the Postwar United States and Mexico*. Chapel Hill: University of North Carolina Press.

Compa, Lance. 2000. *Unfair Advantage: Workers' Freedom of Association in the United States Under International Human Rights Standards*. Ithaca and London: Cornell University Press.

Concheiro Bórquez, Elvira. 1996. *El Gran Acuerdo: Gobierno y empresarios en la modernización salinista*. Mexico City: Universidad Nacional Autónoma de México.

Consejo Coordinador Empresarial. n.d. "El Consejo Coordinador Empresarial." At <cce.org.mx/acerca-de/>.

Consejo Nacional de Evaluación de la Política de Desarrollo Social (CONEVAL). n.d. "Evolucion de la Pobreza por Ingresos a Nivel Nacional." At: <coneval.gob. mx/cmsconeval/rw/resource/coneval/home/2568.pdf>.

Cornelius, Wayne. 1998. "The Structural Embeddedness of Demand for Mexican Immigrant Labor." In Marcelo M. Suárez-Orozco (ed.), *Crossings: Mexican Immigration in Interdisciplinary Perspectives*, 115–44. Cambridge: Harvard University Press.

Cowie, Jefferson. 2010. *Stayin' Alive: The 1970s and the Last Days of the Working Class*. New York: New Press.

____. 1999. *Capital Moves: RCA's 70-Year Quest for Cheap Labor*. Ithaca: Cornell University Press.

Crispo, John. 1967. *International Unionism: A Study in Canadian-American Relations*. Toronto: McGraw Hill.

Curzio, Leonardo. 1998. *La gobernabilidad en el México contemporáneo*. México, D.F.: Fundación CIDOB.

Cypher, James M. 1990. *State and Capital in Mexico*. Boulder, CO: Westview.

Cypher, James M., and Raúl Delgado Wise. 2010. *Mexico's Economic Dilemma: The Developmental Failure of Neoliberalism*. Lanham: Rowman and Littlefield.

Davies, Charles. 1977. "Blue Chip Roster for Business Council." *Board of Trade Journal*. April. At <lib.uwo.ca/programs/generalbusiness/bcni.html>.

Department of Homeland Security. 2011. *Yearbook of Immigration Statistics*. Office of Immigration Statistics.

Dion, Michelle. 2008. "Retrenchment, Expansion and the Transformation of Mexican

Social Protection Policies." *Social Policy and Administration* 42, 4 (August).

Doern, G. Bruce, and Brian Tomlin. 1991. *Faith and Fear: The Free Trade Story*. Toronto: Stoddart.

Dunn, Timothy J. 1996. *The Militarization of the U.S.–Mexico Border, 1978–1992*. Austin: University of Texas Press.

Emery, Kathy, and Susan Ohanian. 2004. *Why Is Corporate America Bashing Our Public Schools?* Portsmouth, NH: Heinemann.

Fantasia, Rick. 1988. *Cultures of Solidarity: Consciousness, Action, and Contemporary American Workers*. Berkeley and Los Angeles: University of California Press.

Faux, Jeff. 2006. *The Global Class War: How America's Bipartisan Elite Lost Our Future — And What It Will Take to Win It Back*. Hoboken, NJ: John Wiley.

Ferguson, Thomas, and Joel Rogers. 1986. *Right Turn: The Decline of the Democrats and the Future of American Politics*. New York: Hill and Wang.

Fitzpatrick-Behrens, Susan. 2009. "Plan Mexico and Central American Migration." *NACLA (North American Congress on Latin America)* January 12. At <http://nacla.org/node/5406>.

Forbes Magazine. n.d. "The World's Billionaires." At <forbes.com/billionaires/list/>.

Frundt, Henry. 2000. "Models of Cross-Border Organizing in Maquila Industries." *Critical Sociology* 26, 1–2 (July): 36-55.

Gabaccia, Donna R. 2004. "Constructing North America: Railroad Building and the Rise of Continental Migrations, 1850-1914." In Marc C. Rodriguez (ed.), *Repositioning North American Migration History*. Rochester: University of Rochester Press.

Gasparello, Giovanna. 2009. "Policía Comunitaria de Guerrero, investigación y autonomía." *Política y Cultura* 32: 61–78.

Gerstle, Gary. 1989. *Working-Class Americanism: The Politics of Labor in a Textile City, 1914–1960*. Cambridge: Cambridge University Press.

Gibson, Campbell, and Kay Jung. 2006. "Historical Census Statistics on the Foreign-Born Population of the United States." Washington. DC: U.S. Census Bureau.

Gindin, Sam. 1995. *The Canadian Auto Workers: The Birth and Transformation of a Union*. Toronto: James Lorimer.

___. 2004. *The Auto Industry — Concretizing Working Class Solidarity: Internationalism Beyond Slogans*. Toronto: Socialist Project. At <http://socialistproject.ca/documents/The%20Auto%20Industry.pdf>.

González, Alfonso. 2009. "The 2006 *Mega Marchas* in Greater Los Angeles: Counter-Hegemonic Moment and The Future of *El Migrante* Struggle." *Latino Studies* 7: 30-59.

Grayson, George W. 2007. *The Mexico–U.S. Business Committee: Catalyst for the North American Free Trade Agreement*. Rockville, MA: Montrose.

Greenspan, Alan. 2000. "Structural Change in the New Economy." Remarks to the National Governors' Association, 92nd Annual Meeting, State College, Pennsylvania, July 11. Federal Reserve Board. At <federalreserve.gov/boarddocs/speeches/2000/20000711.htm>.

Grieco, Elizabeth M., et al. 2012. "The Size, Place of Birth, and Geographic Distribution of the Foreign-Born Population in the United States: 1960 to

References

2010." Population Division Working Paper No. 96. Washington, DC: U.S. Census Bureau.

Gross, James R. 1995. *Broken Promise: The Subversion of U.S. Labor Relations Policy, 1947–1994.* Philadelphia: Temple University Press.

Gutiérrez, David G. 1995. *Walls and Mirrors: Mexican Americans, Mexican Immigrants, and the Politics of Ethnicity.* Berkeley: University of California Press.

Hansen, Marcus Lee. 1940. *The Mingling of the Canadian and American Peoples.* New Haven: Yale University Press.

Hathaway, Dale. 2000. *Allies Across the Border: Mexico's "Authentic Labor Front" and Global Solidarity.* Cambridge: South End Press.

Hellman, Judith Adler. 1983. *Mexico in Crisis.* Second ed. New York and London: Holmes and Meier.

Heron, Craig. 1996. *The Canadian Labour Movement: A Short History.* Toronto: James Lorimer and Company.

Heyman, Josiah McC. 1991. *Life and Labor on the Border.* Tucson: University of Arizona Press.

Immigration and Naturalization Service (INS), U.S. and Secretaría de Relaciones Exteriores, Mexico. 1992. "Migration between Mexico and the United States."

IMSS (Instituto Mexicano del Seguro Social). 2010a. *Memoria estadística del IMSS. Capítulo Evolución del Empleo.* México, DF: Insituto Mexicano del Seguro Social.

___. 2010b. *Memoria estadística del IMSS, Insituto Mexicano del Seguro Social, 2010.* Capítulo Evolución de los trabajadores cotizantes por Nivel de Ingreso. México, DF.

INEGI (Instituto Nacional de Estadística y Geografía). 2009. *Encuesta Nacional de Ingreso Gasto de los Hogares 2008 Ampliada Cuadro XX Característica de los Ingresos por Rubro.* México, DF: INEGI.

___. 2012. *Cuaderno de Información Oportuna Regional.* Segundo Trimestre del año 2012. cuadro 3.11. México, DF: INEGI

International Labour Organization. 2005. *Trade Union Membership and Collective Bargaining Coverage: Statistical Concepts, Methods and Findings.* Working Paper No. 59 (October). Geneva: International Labour Organization.

Inwood, Gregory J. 2005. *Continentalizing Canada: The Politics and Legacy of the Macdonald Royal Commission.* Toronto: University of Toronto Press.

Jameson, Stuart. 1973. *Industrial Relations in Canada.* Second ed. Toronto: Macmillan of Canada.

Johns, Rebecca A. 1998. "Bridging the Gap between Class and Space: U.S. Worker Solidarity with Guatemala." *Economic Geography* 74, 3: 252–71.

Kanstroom, Daniel. 2007. *Deportation Nation: Outsiders in American History.* Cambridge: Harvard University Press.

Kay, Tamara. 2011. *NAFTA and the Politics of Labor Transnationalism.* Cambridge: Cambridge University Press.

Kearney, Michael. 1991. "Borders and Boundaries of State and Self at the End of Empire." *Journal of Historical Sociology* 4: 52–74.

Kelleher, Christian. 2006–07. "Benson Collection Archive Documents: Roots of NAFTA Development." Portal 2. At <lanic.utexas.edu/project/etext/llilas/portal/portal079/benson.pdf>.

Kimeldorf, Howard. 1999. *Battling for American Labor: Wobblies, Craft Workers and the Making of the Union Movement.* Berkeley and Los Angeles: University of California Press.

Kochhar, Rakesh. 2012. "Labor Force Growth Slows, Hispanic Share Grows." *Pew Social and Demographic Trends.* February 13. At <pewsocialtrends.org/2012/02/13/labor-force-growth-slows-hispanic-share-grows-2/>.

Kopinak, Kathryn, and Rosa Maria Soriano Miras. 2010. "Maquiladora Employment in Mexico and Labor Migration to the U.S.: The Impact of the Crisis." Paper presented at the Latin American Studies Association Conference on Crisis, Response, and Recovery in Toronto, Canada on October 8.

La Botz, Dan. 1992. *Mask of Democracy: Labor Suppression in Mexico Today.* Boston: South End Press.

___. 2010a. "United Steel Workers and Mineros Explore Merger." *Mexican Labor News and Analysis* 15, 5 (July).

___. 2010b. "USW Hails Mexican Superior Court Decision Vindicating Los Mineros Leader Napoleon Gomez." *Mexican Labor News and Analysis* 15, 5 (July).

La Jornada. 2011. "Periodistas Asesinados en México desde el año 2000." September 2. At <jornada.unam.mx/2011/09/02/politica/007n2pol>.

Lacey, Marc. 2009. "Money Trickles North as Mexicans Help Relatives." *New York Times*, November 15.

Langille, David. 1987. "The Business Council on National Issues and the Canadian State." *Studies in Political Economy* 24: 41–85.

Lantigua. John. 2011. "Illegal Immigrants Pay Social Security Tax, Won't Benefit." *The Seattle Times*, December 28.

Leahy, Dan. 2010. "A Brief History of the Trinational Coalition." At <trinationalcoalition.org/index_en.html>.

Leland, John. 2006. "Immigrants Stealing U.S. Social Security Numbers for Jobs, not Profits." *New York Times*, September 4.

Lichtenstein, Nelson. 2002. *State of the Union: A Century of American Labor.* Princeton: Princeton University Press.

Linder, Marc. 2000. *Wars of Attrition: Vietnam, the Business Roundtable, and the Decline of Construction Unions.* Second ed. Iowa City: Fanpihua.

López Obrador, Andrés Manuel. 2007. *La mafia nos robó la Presidencia.* México: Grijalbo.

MacArthur, John R. 2000. *The Selling of "Free Trade:" NAFTA, Washington, and the Subversion of American Democracy.* New York: Hill and Wang.

Maddison, Angus. 2001 *The World Economy: A Millennial Perspective.* Paris: OECD.

Marier, Patrik. "The Changing Conception of Pension Rights in Canada, Mexico and the United States." *Social Policy and Administration* 42, 4 (August).

Marois, Thomas. 2008. "The 1982 Mexican Bank Statization and the Unintended Consequences for the Emergence of Neoliberalism." *Canadian Journal of Political Science* 41, 1: 143–67.

Mayer, Frederick W. 1998. *Interpreting NAFTA: The Science and Art of Political Analysis.* New York: Columbia University Press.

McBride, Stephen. 2005. *Paradigm Shift: Globalization and the Canadian State.* Black Point, NS: Fernwood.

McCormack, A. Ross. 1975. "The Industrial Workers of the World in Western Canada, 1905–1914." Historical Papers, Canadian Historical Association.

McKay, Jim. 2011. "USW, Los Mineros Strengthen Alliance." USW Communications.

References

At <assets.usw.org/convention-11/daily-newsletter/USW-Update-tuesday.pdf>.

Meier, Matt S. and Feliciano Ribera. 1993. *Mexican Americans/American Mexicans.* United States: Hill and Wang.

Mellinger, Philip J. 1995. *Race and Labor in Western Copper: The Fight for Equality, 1896–1918.* Tucson: University of Arizona Press.

Middlebrook, Kevin J. 1995. *The Paradox of Revolution: Labor, the State, and Authoritarianism in Mexico.* Baltimore: Johns Hopkins University Press.

Milkman, Ruth L.A. 2006. *L.A. Story: Immigrant Workers and the Future of the U.S. Labor Movement.* New York: Russell Sage Foundation.

Montejano. David. 1987. *Anglos and Mexicans in the Making of Texas, 1836–1986.* Austin: University of Texas Press.

National Security Archive, George Washington University. 2006. *The Dead of Tlatelolco: Using the Archives to Exhume the Past.* National Security Archive Electronic Briefing Book No. 201. Washington, DC: National Security Archive. At <http://www.gwu.edu/~nsarchiv/NSAEBB/NSAEBB201/index.htm>.

New America Media. 2012. "Future of Anti-Immigrant State Laws on the Line for 2012." At <newamericamedia.org/2012/01/future-of-anti-immigrant-state-laws-on-the-line-for-2012.php>.

Pallares, Amalia, and Nilda Flores-González. 2010. *¡Marcha! Latino Chicago and the Immigrant Rights Movement.* Urbana: University of Illinois Press.

Passel Jeffrey, and D'Vera Cohn. 2008. "US Population Projections: 2005–2050." Washington, DC: Pew Research Center.

___. 2011. "Unauthorized Immigrant Population: National and State Trends, 2010." Washington, DC: Pew Research Center. February 1. At <http://www.pewhispanic.org/2011/02/01/unauthorized-immigrant-population-brnational-and-state-trends-2010/>.

Peck, Jamie. 1996. *Work Place: The Social Regulation of Labor Markets.* New York: Guilford Press.

Phillips-Fein, Kim. 2009. *Invisible Hands: The Businessmen's Crusade Against the New Deal.* New York: W.W. Norton

Poder Ejecutivo Federal. 2010. *IV Informe de Gobierno.* México, DF: Government of Mexico.

Poniatowska, Elena. 1975. *Massacre in Mexico.* New York: Viking Press.

Porter, Eduardo. 2005. "Illegal Immigrants Are Bolstering Social Security with Billions." *New York Times,* April 5.

Puga, Cristina. 2004. *Los empresarios organizados y el Tratado de Libre Comercio de América del Norte.* Mexico City: Universidad Nacional Autónoma de México.

Ramirez, Bruno. 1991. *On the Move: French-Canadian and Italian Migrants in the North Atlantic Economy, 1860–1914.* Toronto: McClelland and Stewart.

___. 2001. "Canada in the United States: Perspectives on Migration and Continental History." *Journal of American Ethnic History* 20, 3 (Spring): 50–70.

___. 2004. "Borderland Studies and Migration: The Canada/United States Case." In Marc C. Rodriguez (ed.), *Repositioning North American Migration History.* Rochester: University of Rochester Press.

Raphael, Ricardo. 2007. *Los Socios de Elba Esther.* Mexico: Planeta.

Rasmus, Jack. 2006. *The War at Home: The Corporate Offensive from Ronald Reagan to George W. Bush.* San Ramon, CA: Kyklos.

Reimers, David M. 1992. *Still the Golden Door: The Third World Comes to America.* New York: Columbia University Press.

Ribando Seelke, Clare. 2009. "Mérida Initiative for Mexico and Central America: Funding and Policy Issues." Congressional Research Service Report. Washington, DC. At <http://www.fas.org/sgp/crs/row/R40135.pdf>.

Robinson, Ian. 2002. "The International Dimension of Labour Federation Economic Strategy in Canada and the United States, 1947–2000." In Jeffrey Harrod and Robert O'Brien (eds), *Global Unions? Theory and Strategies of Organized Labour in the Global Political Economy.* London: Routledge.

Rodriguez, Rolando B. 2001. La Prensa de Panamá. Panama, June 21.

Roediger, David R. 1999. *The Wages of Whiteness: Race and the Making of the American Working Class.* New York: Verso.

____. 2005. *Working Toward Whiteness: How America's Immigrants Became White.* New York: Basic Books.

Roman, Richard. 1976. *Ideología y Clase en la Revolución.* Mexico: Sepsetentas, Secretaría de Educación Pública.

Roman, Richard, and Edur Velasco Arregui. 2009. *Mexico: The Murder of a Union and the Rebirth of Class Struggle.* "Part I: The New Assault." November 25. At <socialistproject.ca/bullet/279.php>; "Part II: The Fightback." November 26. At <socialistproject.ca/bullet/280.php>.

____. 2007. "Mexico's Oaxaca Commune." In Leo Panitch and Colin Leys (eds), *Socialist Register 2008: Global Flashpoints: Reactions to Imperialism and Neoliberalis.* London: Merlin Press.

____. 2012a. "The New Student Rebellion and the Mexican Left: Challenging the Corporate Media and the Electoral Fraud." Socialist Project • E-Bulletin 673, August 1. At <http://www.socialistproject.ca/bullet/673.php>.

____. 2012b. "Neoliberal Authoritarianism, the 'Democratic Transition' and the Mexican Left." In Barry Carr and Jeff Webber (eds.), *The New Latin American Left: Cracks in the Empire.* Lanham: Rowman and Littlefield.

Ross, Robert J.S., and Kent C. Trachte. 1990. *Global Capitalism: The New Leviathan.* Albany: State University of New York Press.

Sassen, Saskia. 1996. "U.S. Immigration Policy Toward Mexico in a Global Economy." In David G. Gutiérrez (ed.), *Between Two Worlds.* Wilmington: Scholarly Resources.

Schneider, Ben Ross. 2002. "Why Is Mexican Business So Organized?" *Latin American Research Review* 37, 1: 77–118.

Selfa, Lance. 2008. *The Democrats: A Critical History.* Chicago: Haymarket.

Sklair, Leslie. 1989. *Assembling for Development.* Boston: Unwin Hyman.

Smith, Miriam. 1992. "The Canadian Labour Congress: From Continentalism to Economic Nationalism." *Studies in Political Economy* 38, Summer: 35–60.

Stevens, Evelyn P. 1974. *Protest and Response in Mexico.* Cambridge, MA: MIT Press.

Thacker, Strom C. 2000. *Big Business, the State and Free Trade: Constructing Coalitions in Mexico.* Cambridge: Cambridge University Press.

Thompson, E.P. 1966. *The Making of the English Working Class.* New York: Vintage.

United Nations Population Fund. 2011. *The State of World Population 2011.* New York: UNFPA.

U.S. Census Bureau. 1996. Statistical Abstract of the U.S. Washington, DC: U.S.

References

Census Bureau.

___. 2011a. "American Community Survey, Select Characteristics of Foreign Born Population." Washington, DC: U.S. Census Bureau. At <http://www.census.gov/acs/www>.

___. 2011b. "Current Population Survey (CPS), 2010 Poverty Table of Contents." Washington, DC: U.S. Census Bureau. At <census.gov/hhes/www/cpstables/032011/pov/POV01_100.htm>.

___. 2011c. "Hispanics 2010." Census Bureau Briefs. Washington, DC: U.S. Census Bureau.

___. 2011d. *Historical Poverty Data*. Washington, DC: U.S. Census Bureau.

___. 2011e. *Income, Poverty, and Health Insurance Coverage in the United States: 2010*. Washington, DC: U.S. Census Bureau.

___. 2011f. "Population and Area 1790 to 2010." Population 8, Table 1. Washington, DC: U.S. Census Bureau.

___. 2011g. *"Rooms, Size, and Amenities — Renter-Occupied Units (National)* 2011 American Housing Survey." Washington, DC: U.S. Census Bureau. At <factfinder2.census.gov/faces/tableservices/jsf/pages/productview.xhtml?pid=AHS_2011_C02RO&prodType=table>.

___. 2012a. "Income, Poverty and Health Insurance Coverage." September, page 8, Table 2. Washington, DC: U.S. Census Bureau. At <census.gov/prod/2012pubs/p60-243.pdf>.

___. 2012b. "Statistical Abstract of the United States 2012." Table 23, Population section, 31. Washington, DC: U.S. Census Bureau.

Valdés Ugalde, Francisco. 1997. *Autonomía y Legitimidad: Los empresarios, la política y el estado en México*. Mexico, DF: Siglo Veintuno Editores.

Vargas, Zaragoza. 1998. "Rank and File: Historical Perspectives on Latino/a Workers in the U.S." In Antonia Darder and Rodolfo D. Torres (eds.), *The Latino Studies Reader*. Oxford: Blackwell.

___. 2011. *Crucible of Struggle: A History of Mexican Americans from Colonial Times to the Present Era*. New York: Oxford University Press.

Velasco, Edur, and Richard Roman. 1998. "Migración, mercados laborales y pobreza en el Septentrión Americano." *Chiapas* 6: 41–68.

Vicario, Elena, Sandra Polaski and Dalil Maschino. 2003. *North American Labor Markets, Main Changes Since NAFTA*. Secretariat of the Commission for Labor Cooperation. At <http://dspace.cigilibrary.org/jspui/handle/123456789/757>.

Vogel, David. 1989. *Fluctuating Fortunes: The Political Power of Business in America*. New York: Basic Books.

Woodward, Bob. 2011. *Greenspan*. Madrid: Editorial Península.

Workman, Thom. 2009. *If You're in My Way, I'm Walking: The Assault on Working People Since 1970*. Halifax: Fernwood Publishing.

Xelhuantzi López, María, et al. 2005. *Auge y Perspectivas de los Contratos de Proteccion*. México: Fundación Friederich Ebert.

Index